The ABCs of Nonprofits

Lisa A. Runquist

Printed in the United States of America.

Library of Congress Cataloging-in-Publication Data

Runquist, Lisa.
 The ABCs of nonprofits / Lisa A. Runquist.
     p. cm.
  ISBN 1-59031-291-0
  1. Nonprofit organizations--Law and legislation--United States. I. Title.

  KF1388.Z9R86 2005
  346.73'064--dc22   2005004119
  ISBN 1-11-159031-1291-10

10 09 08 07 06 05   5 4 3 2 1

Contents

PART III: END OF LIFE PLANNING FOR EXEMPT ORGANIZATIONS

Preface

This book is written as a primer on nonprofit organizations. It is not designed to provide an in-depth analysis on any particular point, but to give the reader an overview of the subject. There are many complex legal issues that have been treated very simply. To those who think it may be too simplistic, my answer is that often people who get involved with nonprofits, even those who are well educated and seemingly sophisticated, are confused about the basic concepts. Unless they can understand these basic concepts, they will never make any headway toward successfully navigating the dangerous rocks that will crop up when least expected. And for those who want more information about a particular subject, numerous publications are available, including several other well-written ABA Business Law Section publications, some of which are listed in Appendix B.

During my years of practice, a number of my clients have asked questions very similar to those that Sam, Pastor Ray, and others ask in this book. I have found it easiest to write as though I were advising Sam or his lawyer. Rather than simply setting forth the law, this book traces Sam's attempt to form and operate his own nonprofit—what works, what doesn't, and why.

I ask the reader's indulgence in my approach, and hope that my attempts at humor will make the end result more readable.

Special thanks should go to my friends, David Pauker, Hildy Gottlieb, Judy Zybach, Stephen Nill, Chris Reeves, Phil Sims, Erle Spencer, and Barnaby Zall, all of who took time out of their busy schedules to review drafts and suggest changes. Their comments have significantly improved the book; any mistakes remain mine.

Introduction

Alvin Lawyer has an old client, Sam Goodman, coming into his office today to get advice on starting a new organization to "Save the Chipmunks." Sam told Alvin that he trusted him and wanted him to handle it. Alvin has always wanted to represent people wearing the white hats, and so he agreed to represent Sam. He has heard that the law affecting nonprofits is complex, but is prepared to spend the time getting up to speed. Where does he start, and what does Sam need to know?

Exempt Status

Nonprofit does not mean tax-exempt. A nonprofit organization can either be taxable or tax-exempt.

An organization can be exempt from income tax under both federal and state law. Sometimes the organization has to actually apply to establish the exempt status with the IRS and/or state taxing authority; in other situations, the organization may be exempt simply by being correctly organized and operated.

There are over 25 different types of organizations that are exempt from income tax on income derived from the organization's exempt purpose. To be exempt, the organization must meet the qualifications required for that particular type of exemption; the organization must be both ORGANIZED and OPERATED for that exempt purpose.

Contributions to the nonprofit are deductible only if they are given to a special type of exempt organization, commonly referred to as a 501(c)(3) organization.

What Is a Nonprofit?—Purpose

Every entity exists for a reason. A business entity exists to ultimately benefit the owners. For example, a corporation exists to benefit the shareholders who own its stock. A nonprofit organization has no owners. Instead, it is formed to promote or advance a specific purpose. This purpose should be carefully defined, as it will control what the nonprofit may or may not do, and it will impact the tax-exempt status of the organization.

Some nonprofit organizations are formed to benefit their members (such as a condominium homeowners association or a social club). These organizations are sometimes referred to as "mutual benefit" organizations. In fact, some of these organizations, even though nonprofit in form, may look a lot like businesses, and the members might look a lot like shareholders. Some mutual benefits may even allow membership interests to be bought and sold. Because the benefit is to the individual(s) and not to society at large, although there may be an exemption from income tax, contributions will not be deductible.

Other nonprofits are formed to indirectly benefit businesses or residents in a particular geographical area, such as a chamber of commerce. Some are formed to benefit a specific type of business or individual, such as professional associations (the American Bar Association and the American Medical Association are two such examples). These organizations may also be exempt from income tax. Contributions to this type of nonprofit may be deductible as a business expense, but again are unlikely to be deductible as a charitable contribution.

If the organization wants to be able to receive tax-deductible contributions, the specific purpose for which it is formed will have to be broad enough to somehow benefit the general public or a significant segment thereof. It cannot be organized or operated for a purpose that benefits only a very limited number of people, even if that purpose is charitable (although such an organization might be exempt from income tax), and it cannot have a primary purpose of benefiting an individual or individuals.

The trick is to draft the purpose so that it is narrow enough to clearly qualify as whatever type of exemption the incorporator wants, while at the same time being broad enough to allow for all expected activities. Alvin might want to suggest to Sam that he consider expanding the purpose of his nonprofit to cover all rodents, and not just chipmunks. On the other hand, "Save the Animals" is probably too broad to satisfy Sam's desires.

Do You Really Want a Nonprofit? —Control Issues

The purpose of a nonprofit organization is *not* to benefit an individual owner or owners. Everything must be done to benefit the purpose of the nonprofit exempt organization.

In order to be tax exempt there may need to be a clear benefit to the public. To assure that the organization is operated for this "nonprofit" purpose, controls are necessary.

One common method to assure such control is to have a board of directors made up of a majority of "independent" or "disinterested" directors. This means that Sam cannot be the only director; he will have to select others to serve with him. Of course, that also means that Sam's ultimate ability to control the organization will be limited. In fact, it may mean that, at some point, Sam will be outvoted, and perhaps even removed from the board.

Some individuals, when they form a nonprofit, do so with a specific vision of what they want to see accomplished, and indeed, without their energy and vision, the nonprofit is unlikely to succeed. However, if the founder is unwilling to share control, serious consideration should be given to whether a nonprofit organization is the correct form of entity.

A further question has to do with whether the founder expects to receive compensation from the organization. In such a situation, it is even more important that the majority of directors of a nonprofit organization be disinterested, to assure that the organization is operated for the nonprofit purpose, rather than for the private benefit of the founder. If an individual having substantial influence over the organization receives a benefit greater than what he or she provides to the organization, the individual may become subject to substantial penalties, and the organization may lose its exempt status.

The fundamental question is will the organization be more effective as a nonprofit, or will its purposes be better served as a business? For example, there are schools run as businesses and schools operated as nonprofits. Both receive a significant amount of funds from tuition; however, only nonprofit schools can also receive tax-deductible contributions. If tax-deductible contributions are necessary to the operation of the organization, a nonprofit may be the only answer. However, if the organization does not need these contributions and the founder wants to maintain complete control over the organization and retain all profits from its activity, he or she might be better served by having a business and forgoing the benefits of nonprofit status.[1]

---

1. For additional thoughts on whether a nonprofit is right for you, see "Get Ready, Get Set" at http://www.cnmsocal.org/Services/p_grgs.html.

Basic Differences and Similarities[2]

	Business	Nonprofit 501(c)(3)	Nonprofit other
Can receive tax deductible charitable contributions	No	Yes	No
Can derive funds from operations	Yes	Yes	Yes
Operated to benefit	Owners	Purpose/ General Public	Purpose
Benefit may be limited to certain individuals	Yes	No	Generally Yes
Can pay reasonable salaries	Yes	Yes	Yes
Profits	Accrue to owner(s)	Must be used for nonprofit, tax—1exempt purpose	Must be used for purpose
Taxed on Income	Yes	No, unless derived from business unrelated to exempt purpose	No, unless derived from business unrelated to purpose
Control	Founder can maintain control	Founder, if compensated, loses control	Depends on organization
Owners/Members	Owners' interests can be sold	Members' interests cannot be sold	Depends on organization
Directors	Often are compensated	Majority uncompensated	Depends on organization
Dissolution	Assets go to owner(s)	Assets go to another charitable entity	Depends on organization

---

2. Note: This chart provides only a basic picture of the similarities and differences; the reality is much more complex. If a particular item is desired, your attorney should be consulted to see if the particular structure works for your organization.

PART I

Forming Your Nonprofit

Choice of Entity

After receiving a brief overview of the nonprofit law, Sam Goodman, now convinced that a nonprofit is indeed a good idea, asks whether he really wants a corporation or whether a different form would be better. He heard that Limited Liability Companies (LLCs) were the newest and greatest form of organization, and wondered if a corporation was not passé. Alvin wisely told Sam he would have to research the issue to see if another form would be better for Sam than the corporate form, since he knew that most nonprofits were corporations. What advice should Alvin give to Sam?

There are currently four different forms of entities that are being used for nonprofits. The following is a summary of these different forms, with a discussion of why one form might be used rather than another.

Trusts

A trust is formed by someone (the trustor) transferring assets to another (the trustee), with the understanding that the trustee will use these assets to benefit some specific purpose or person (the beneficiary). Generally there is a trust instrument that defines who each of these parties are, and what the trustee can and cannot do. When we refer to a "charitable trust," we are generally referring to an actual "trust" entity that has one or more trustees, trust assets, and a charitable purpose for which the trust was formed.

A trust can be formed without obtaining permission from, or filing anything with, a government entity.

Unless modified in the trust instrument, the trustee is generally the person who both makes and implements decisions. The trustee may be an individual or individuals, or it may be a separate entity, such as a bank. The trust instrument should provide for how a new trustee can be chosen if the existing trustee dies or is unwilling or unable to continue as trustee. If the trust instrument does not provide for a term of office, the trustee continues to serve indefinitely.

In the case of a charitable trust, the beneficiaries are not specific individuals. They may be an undefined group of individuals, or the beneficiary may be a purpose unrelated to an individual, (e.g., protection of the environment) where the public good is the ultimate beneficiary.

State law applicable to trusts generally also applies to charitable trusts. A trustee may or may not be able to delegate his or her duties to another, depending both on state law and the language of the trust instrument. A trust may be established as a tax-exempt entity in the same manner as a corporation.

The History of Charitable Trusts

To understand charitable trusts, it is necessary to go back some 400 years, to England. Prior to 1601, trusts could only be formed for the benefit of a particular person. This made it difficult to enforce a trust formed to benefit a purpose if the trustee decided to use the assets for a different purpose. In 1601, England adopted a "Statute of Charitable Uses" which was designed to correct abuses, breaches of trust, and fraud occurring when property was given for charitable purposes. It set forth the purposes for which charitable trusts could be created. The purposes listed in the Statute included the repair of churches; the education of orphans; the relief of aged, impotent, and poor people; the maintenance of schools and university professors; and so forth.

In the early days of the United States, a corporation could only be formed by special act of a legislative body. Rather than pursuing special legislative action to obtain a corporate charter, many opted to use trusts to hold property dedicated to a charitable purpose, using this same "Statute of Charitable Uses" trust concept. Since the formation of a corporation has now become a simple process of filing, most charitable organizations formed today are corporations.

It should be noted that court decisions have applied the charitable trust doctrine to all charitable organizations, both where property is held by an individual in trust for the group, and where the property is in the name of a separate corporation. As a result, this is a confusing area, as a non-trust entity, such as a corporation, may still be described as holding assets "in trust" for a specific purpose.

The question arises as to who can enforce the trust. The simple answer has been that the state, as guardian of the public good, has the right, and the *duty*, to see that the trust is enforced. In many states, it is the Attorney General to whom this right and duty has been assigned. See State Jurisdiction (Attorney General), below.

Corporations

Today, the most common form of nonprofit is the corporation. A corporation is a creature of statute, formed by a person or persons pursuing a common goal or enterprise. To form a corporation, a person (the incorporator) files Articles of Incorporation (sometimes called a Corporate Charter) with the state. The incorporator then elects other people to manage the corporation (the directors), unless the directors are already listed in the Articles. Prior to the selection of the directors, the incorporator may take such other actions as would normally be taken by the directors. However, once the directors are selected, the incorporator's duties end. Bylaws are adopted either by the incorporator or by the initial directors and provide the internal rules by which the corporation functions.

A principal advantage of a corporation over other possible options is that the corporate entity is unquestionably its own "person," distinct from its members, directors, and officers. Moreover, a corporation operates under a clearly defined set of rules of governance and law. Perhaps most importantly, if a corporation is properly formed and operated, it can offer considerable protection from personal liability to its individual directors, officers, members, employees, and volunteers.

The protection from personal liability for persons who act on behalf of corporations is not absolute. For that reason it is generally wise to make sure that the corporation has substantial assets available to pay claims and that applicable insurance coverage is in place.

Care must also be taken to observe proper formalities required when doing business in the corporate form, including management by or under the direction of the Board of Directors and the maintenance of minutes and other corporate records.

In most states, the nonprofit corporate laws are based on similar provisions of the law applicable to business corporations. Initially, the nonprofit law consisted of a few special rules for nonprofit corporations, with the business corporation law of the state otherwise applicable. This has been changing. A number of states have used some form of the Model Nonprofit Corporation Act,[3] which, although it parallels the business law, is a stand-alone law. Generally this has been found preferable because nonprofit enterprises are fundamentally distinguishable from business corporations. It is important to periodically check your state law to make sure you are still in compliance, as both the model act and various state laws are regularly amended.

A principal distinction between a nonprofit and a business is the fact that a business corporation issues shares (to the owners of the company), and generally exists to make a profit for its shareholders. In contrast, a nonprofit corporation has no owners and exists primarily to advance a purpose or objective. Nonprofit corporations are not even required to have a class of members that the organization serves. The goal and focus of the management of charitable organizations should be to advance the entity's stated purposes, rather than the interests of any group of individuals affiliated with the charity.

Unincorporated Associations

An "unincorporated association" is created when two or more people join together to accomplish some purpose. An unincorporated association may be formed simply by two or more people doing something jointly, even if there is no written document defining what they are doing or how they expect to do it. As with a trust, no governmental action is required to form an unincorporated association.

The unincorporated association may choose how it is governed. For example, the members may govern the organization directly, or they may choose others to govern (i.e., directors). This is both one of the advantages and one of the detriments of

---

3. The Model Nonprofit Corporation Act (1964) and the Revised Model Nonprofit Corporation Act (1987) were both drafted by the American Bar Association, Business Law Section. The Act is currently in the process of being revised to take into account changes in corporate law since the last revision.

an unincorporated association. The structure is very flexible and can be designed in whatever manner is desired. However, because of this flexibility, it is important that a design be chosen, unlike a corporation where the design is statutorily required.

The idea of an unincorporated association, which is formed without the permission of the state, is actually even older than the trust. Roman civil law allowed an entity to be formed simply by the voluntary consent of the members, without special approval by the government. Unincorporated associations today are equivalent to these voluntary civil law corporations, which do not require special act of the King, Parliament, Congress, or anyone else; whereas the corporate form is a simplified version of the English corporation, which could only exist with the consent of the King. The ability to have an association, apart from the specific consent of the government, could be argued to be guaranteed under the First Amendment to the Constitution protecting freedom of association.

There may be a question of whether or not an unincorporated association is a legal entity apart from its members. As noted above, two essential elements of an unincorporated association are the voluntary joining *and* a joining to serve a common or agreed purpose or objective. If the organization is charitable, its purpose or objective will not be to benefit any of the individuals involved, but rather to benefit the charitable purpose. Thus, the members join only because of their concern for the purpose, and not to achieve anything for themselves. Indeed, if the organization is to be exempt as a charity, members *cannot* receive something for themselves. Because of this, it is appropriate for an unincorporated association formed for charitable purposes to be considered as an entity apart from any of the individuals involved.

On the other hand, if the nonprofit unincorporated association is not charitable—for example, if it were a homeowners association, a social club, or a co-op—it might be argued that the members are really more like partners. However, even here, it is likely that the existence of the organization is not dependent upon the involvement of any particular individual; therefore, holding the unincorporated association to be an entity is more reasonable.

The Uniform Nonprofit Unincorporated Associations Act, drafted by The National Conference of Commissioners on Uniform State Laws[4] and adopted by some states, does regard the association as a separate entity. And in some states, such as California, statutory law has considered an unincorporated association to be a legal entity for at least some purposes. However, in states that do not have a statutory unincorporated association law, the association may be considered to be the members (similar to a partnership, which is not separate from its partners). This can result in personal liability to the members for actions taken by or on behalf of the unincorporated association. Alvin should make sure he understands the law in his state before he recommends the use of an unincorporated association. He also needs to make sure he fully explains the risks of using this type of entity.

Exempt status can be established for an unincorporated association, just as with a trust and a corporation.

---

4. The National Conference of Commissioners on Uniform State Laws (NCCUSL), now 112 years old, is made up of lawyers who are appointed by each state to draft uniform legislation. After NCCUSL approves a "uniform law," states then consider whether to adopt it, in whole or in part. Its most successful "uniform law" is the Uniform Commercial Code that has been adopted in all 50 states.

There are several different types of situations where unincorporated associations may be utilized. The first, and most common, is a situation where the individuals involved in the organization are not sophisticated, and the organization is quite small. An example of this would be a garden club that meets occasionally, collects dues, and has a small bank account. In this situation, the organization is simply not big enough to warrant incorporation, nor are the people sophisticated enough to have thought about what steps they might take if they were to incorporate. Because they do not have any real property and do not have substantial expenses requiring major fund-raising, there is no major incentive to incorporate. One reason that has been used for not incorporating this type of entity is that it is likely that such a group would fail to comply with the corporate formalities within a few years or would forget to make a required filing, and would thus lose its corporate status and revert to being an unincorporated entity anyway.

The second type of unincorporated association is an organization that has deliberately chosen to maintain itself in an unincorporated form. This type of organization is likely to have written documents, such as articles of association and bylaws, and might well have applied for and obtained an exempt status. For example, some churches have specifically determined that they are religiously opposed to obtaining authorization for their existence from a state, and therefore refuse to adopt a corporate structure. Further, the corporate governance structure is inflexible; if an organization wants a structure that does not fall under the normal corporate structure, it may not be able to use a corporation.

The third type of unincorporated association is an entity that, for one reason or another, is unable to operate in a corporate format. For example, if a joint venture is to occur between an American charity and a Canadian charity, it cannot be incorporated in one of the states without violating the provisions of Revenue Canada. Therefore, any such joint venture can only occur as an unincorporated association.

Limited Liability Companies

A form of business entity that has recently become popular is the limited liability company (LLC). An LLC is similar to an unincorporated association but with a statutory framework defining its organization and operation. Each state has its own LLC law. The LLC is formed by filing Articles of Organization or similar document with the state. Many states specifically allow an LLC to be formed for nonprofit purposes; others require a business purpose.

LLCs were first developed as an alternative to a partnership form. All partners (owners and participants) of a general partnership have unlimited liability. A limited partnership allows the investors (limited partners) to have limited liability, but requires the manager (general partner) to have unlimited liability. An LLC has limited liability for both the investors and the managers as does a corporation, but it can be taxed as a partnership. This limited liability is clearly one reason that a nonprofit LLC might be preferred over an unincorporated association.

As with unincorporated associations, LLCs have much more leeway to choose how they are organized and governed than do corporations. For example, an organization may wish to be governed directly by the members, rather than having a separate board of directors. The only other alternative would be to form an unincorporated association without the statutory framework and protections of an LLC, which, as we have noted, may result in personal liability for the members.

Most states now allow an LLC to be formed with only one member, unlike the unincorporated association that requires the joining together of more than one person.

Some or all of the members may manage the LLC directly (a managing member) or the members may select others to manage the LLC (managers). The managers of an LLC are like the directors of a corporation, except that they have only the power that has been given to them by the members in the Articles of Organization, or in the operating agreement (which functions as the internal rules for the organization, like the bylaws of a corporation).

An LLC can elect to be taxed either as a corporation or as a partnership. The IRS has found partnerships to be business entities. However, if an LLC elects to be taxed as a corporation and meets the other requirements for exemption, it should be able to establish its exempt status separately. In September of 2000,[5] the IRS decided that an LLC may be tax exempt as a separate entity if its membership is composed of other exempt organizations and other requirements are met. The IRS has not addressed the ability of an LLC with individual members (such as a congregational church) to be tax exempt.

If the LLC has only one member and the LLC does not elect corporate tax treatment, then the LLC will be a disregarded entity (it will be considered to be a part of the parent entity for tax purposes), although its structure will still allow for limited liability for organizational and operational purposes. Therefore, if the one member is tax exempt, then it is not necessary to file a separate exemption application for the LLC.

From the standpoint of the parent nonprofit, the LLC may have an advantage over a separate controlled nonprofit corporation for two reasons. The first, as noted above, is that the exempt status may be automatic rather than requiring a separate exemption application filing. The second is that the managers of an LLC may make decisions based on what is best for the parent organization, disregarding what might be best for the LLC as a stand-alone entity. However, in many states, the directors of a nonprofit corporation must make decisions based on what is best for that corporation rather than what might be best for the parent organization.

There are drawbacks to using LLCs. The first is that some states do not clearly allow LLCs to be formed for nonprofit purposes, referring instead to a business purpose. Therefore, it may be necessary to form the LLC in a state that allows an LLC to be formed for nonprofit purposes, and then qualify it to do business in the state in which it will operate.

Secondly, state law may not make it clear that the LLC can be exempt from real property taxation, especially if the LLC has not separately established its exempt status (e.g., it is not clear that the exempt status of the parent extends down to the LLC for purposes of state law issues).

As noted above, a benefit of an LLC over a corporation is that governance provisions may be designed and redesigned to fit the structure desired. But it also

---

5. See *Topic B, Limited Liability Companies as Exempt Organizations—Update;* 2000 (for 2001) *Exempt Organizations CPE Technical Instruction Program Textbook.*

means that how the LLC will operate should be spelled out in detail, if a structure that varies from the default provisions is desired.

A further issue that is unresolved is whether or not a contribution to an LLC that has not separately established its exempt status will be deductible as a charitable contribution, as it would if it were given directly to the parent organization.

The biggest drawback for many entities that might otherwise consider an LLC form is that while the form itself is very flexible, the IRS so far has limited its recognition of exempt status to those LLCs that have membership limited to other exempt organizations. This limitation prevents organizations with nonexempt members from choosing the LLC form to achieve the desired method of governance.

As these issues are resolved, it is much more likely that the LLC will become a more favored form for nonprofits. It is likely that the limited liability company form will be widely used for certain situations that call for potential liability to be split off from the parent organization (such as with the holding of real property). However, for a new nonprofit starting out today, the LLC is unlikely to be the recommended form.

Choosing an Entity

A corporation is the organization with which most people are familiar. Because it is familiar, it is often easier for people to understand. In addition, a corporation is the easiest to form. The articles of incorporation of most nonprofits are only a few pages long and contain only those specific items required by state and federal law. Unless the incorporators want unusual provisions, the only creative part of drafting the articles is generally the purpose clause-making the purpose broad enough to cover all the operations that may be anticipated by the organization, yet narrow enough to make it clear it is organized for charitable, exempt purposes. Statutory law automatically gives the corporation the other powers it needs, so they do not have to be specifically listed in the articles.

Trusts, unincorporated associations, and limited liability companies all require much more extensive drafting of the organizational documents. This is for two reasons: 1) both statutory and case law applicable to these organizations are more limited and do not spell out the powers of the organization, requiring that these powers be stated in the organizational document; 2) similarly, the corporate form is highly regulated in structure (e.g., it requires a board of directors, officers, regular meetings, etc.), whereas all three of the other forms can vary significantly in their method of governance.

A corporation requires that directors be elected on a regular basis. If there are members, directors are normally elected by the members. If there are no members, directors are normally self-perpetuating, i.e. they elect themselves. The terms cannot be open ended. If no term is specified in the organizational documents, the directors are elected annually. In addition, most nonprofit corporations have at least three directors, sometimes significantly more. Sometimes this is required by state law, and sometimes it is necessary or advisable to assure a majority of disinterested directors as may be required under federal or state law, or to obtain the exempt status of the organization. Directors make policy decisions, but delegate the actual operation to the officers.

A trust does not generally require that trustees be elected or replaced. The trustee(s) serve indefinite terms unless the trust specifies otherwise. Often there is only one trustee, although there may be more.

The trustee both makes and implements the decisions, unless this power is modified by the trust.

In LLCs and unincorporated associations, the terms of directors or their equivalents (e.g., managers) are controlled by the organizational documents; or, if no written organizational documents exist in the case of unincorporated associations, by the practice of the organization. Often there is only one manager of an LLC, although there may be more.

A trust is the least flexible when a change in purpose or operation is desired. It is often easier to amend the purpose of a corporation, unincorporated association, or LLC, than to amend the terms of a trust. Because of this, a corporate form may be preferred over a trust if the entity is conducting programs. If the entity is simply managing funds and making grants, a trust entity might be equally as good or better.

Although there may be the ability to waive the strict trust standard, trustees are generally held to a stricter standard of liability than directors or managers of corporations, LLCs, or unincorporated associations. The directors of both business and nonprofit corporations owe a fiduciary duty to their shareholders or members, as well as to the corporation. However, it is well established that a strict trustee standard of duty, which would prohibit any self-dealing, regardless of the benefit conferred, is generally not what is intended or required by most state corporate laws. "A trustee is uniformly held to a high standard of care and will be held liable for simple negligence, while a director must have committed 'gross negligence' or otherwise be guilty of more than mere mistakes in judgment." [6]

From a strict liability standard, a corporation is probably preferable today.

Summary of Entities

	Corporation	Charitable Trust	Unincorporated Association	Limited Liability Company
Government filing required to form	Yes	No	No	Yes
Documents required for formation	Articles of Incorporation, Bylaws	Trust Document	None needed; articles of association and/or bylaws recommended	Articles of Organization or similar document required; Operating Agreement recommended
Easy to amend organizational documents	Yes	No	Generally yes; depends on what is provided in documents or by practice	Yes

---

6. *Stern v. Lucy Webb Hayes School*, 1974, 381 F.Supp. 1033.

	Corporation	Charitable Trust	Unincorporated Association	Limited Liability Company
Governance structure is statutorily defined	Yes	No	No	Default provisions, but can be modified
Governance structure can be varied at will	No	Yes	Yes	Yes
Formalities required (meetings, minutes, etc.)	Yes	No, but recommended	No, but recommended	No, but recommended
Exempt status can be established	Yes	Yes	Yes	Yes, if all members are tax exempt
Entity is separate from members, directors, officers, trustees, etc.	Yes	Yes	Depends on state law	Yes for purposes of liability; depends on election of organization for tax purposes
Members required	No	No	Yes	Yes
Who is responsible for management (making policy decisions)	Directors	Trustees	Determined by organization	Managers or Members as specified by documents
Directors/Managers/ Trustees may have liability for acts	Yes	Yes	Yes	Yes
Liability may be waived	Depends on state law	No	Depends on state law	Depends on state law
Directors/Trustees/ Managers serve indefinite terms	No	Yes	Depends on structure of entity	Depends on structure of entity
Who is responsible for operations (implementing policy decisions)	Officers	Trustees	Determined by organization	Managers or members, as specified by documents
Attorney General has jurisdiction	Yes	Yes	Yes	Yes
Law is well established	Yes	Yes	No	No

Differences in State Laws

"Well," said Sam, "it appears that an LLC may not be the way to go at this time. I guess I will use a corporation. What about incorporating in another state—such as Delaware? Don't most corporations incorporate there?"

Aha! Something Alvin does know about. "Sam," Alvin said, "You have to remember that we are talking about a nonprofit corporation. It is true that many of the large national and international business corporations have chosen Delaware as their state of incorporation; but that is because the law there has been specifically crafted to be beneficial to businesses, and they have an experienced judiciary. But just because a law is good for business, it is not necessarily the law to which you want to be subject as a nonprofit."

"What state would you pick?" Sam asked.

No clear-cut answer exists at this time. It really depends upon the organization and what it finds important. For example, the provisions on indemnification and volunteer protection laws vary substantially from state to state. If Sam is concerned about possible liability, there are some states that he probably would not choose. And there are some differences in the governance provisions of the various states that might be of concern, depending upon the proposed operations. For example, most states require that directors act either at a meeting or by unanimous written consent (they all must sign). If Sam is going to choose a director who may not be available without substantial notice and he needs to get quick turnaround respons- es from the directors, he might want to consider whether a state that requires only majority written consent would better suit his needs.

In talking further to Sam, Alvin notes that the initial operations of the corpora- tion are going to be in Sam's home state of X. If Sam were to choose state Y to use, then he would probably also have to file as a "foreign" corporation in the state of X, and he might well end up having to comply with the laws of both X and Y. He would have filing fees and filings due in both states.

Sam agreed that since he was, at least initially, only going to be operating in the state of X, his life would be less complex if he incorporated there. Alvin agreed that he would check whether there was anything particularly egregious about the state law as it applied to Sam's nonprofit.

Of course, if Sam were going to be operating in several different states, which would require registration to do business in each state, it might be worthwhile to review the law of those particular states before making a final decision. One thing to note is that many states have now adopted some form of the Model Nonprofit Corporation Act. This makes the laws in those states easier to compare.

Forming the Corporation

"Okay," says Sam. "Let's get started! What should we do first?" I have some docu- ments that my brother-in-law, Joe, used when he set up his nonprofit. Can we just use those documents and change the name?

"Oh no, Sam" Alvin replied. "Each nonprofit is different. Although some of the language may look like it is 'cookie cutter' language, you need to look at how your specific nonprofit is going to be organized, managed, and operated. Because there are so many options for nonprofits, it would be much easier and more cost effec- tive to start fresh, rather than to try and modify what someone else has done which may have a structure totally different from what you want."

Where, then, should Sam begin?

Although we have divided the process into a number of steps, as Sam is about to find out, the final product of each step will require decisions to be made about other steps. For example, there are some provisions that may have to be included in the Articles in order to establish the type of exempt status Sam wants. Therefore, Sam will first need to review the entire process and make the major decisions about each step before any documents are finalized.

FIRST STEP: Articles of Incorporation

The first thing Sam needs to do is to draft the Articles of Incorporation (sometimes called a Certificate of Incorporation) and file them with the state (generally with the Secretary of State). This is the "birth certificate" of the corporation; until filed, the corporation does not exist. The exact form differs by State.

Name of Corporation

The name of the corporation should be carefully considered. The name can be descriptive of the purpose, such as the name Sam has initially chosen, "Save the "Chipmunks." It may be a name that would imply the purpose, such as the use of the name "John Muir" as part of the name of an environmental organization. Or it may have no direct connotation of the purpose at all, although if the organization is successful the name will ultimately come to be identified with the purpose. Most states do *not* require the use of "Inc.," "Incorporated," or "Corporation" as part of the corporate name, although some states require a modifier if the rest of the name is not clearly that of a separate entity, so as not to be misleading. For example, in those states the name "Sam Goodman" would not be allowed, although "Sam Goodman Foundation" would. If Sam had decided to use an LLC rather than a corporation, he would have to use "LLC" or "Limited Liability Company" or a similar modifier as part of the name.

Sam wants a name that is different from other entities, so that there is no confusion. It is good practice to check on name availability with the Secretary of State, and to reserve the desired name, if available, as soon as a name is chosen. The Secretary of State will not file the Articles if the name is too similar to a name being used by another organization incorporated in the state.

In addition, Sam will want to make sure that he is not using a name for which someone has already obtained a trademark or service mark registration for a similar purpose. The Patent and Trademark Office website is a good place to check.

Note: Just because a name is registered for use as a trademark or service mark does not mean it is necessarily unavailable. If a trademark or service mark is not actually in use, the rights can be lost, even after registration is obtained.

Purpose Clause

The most important part of the Articles of Incorporation is the purpose clause. It should be narrow enough to distinguish the organization from other nonprofits, but broad enough to allow the organization to accomplish its objectives. The purpose clause generally does not specify the methods by which the organization will carry out the objectives, except, perhaps, in very broad terms.

Sam should be aware that if he makes his purpose clause too narrow, he might be limiting the ability of his organization to operate in the future. For example, the nonprofit operated by Sam's brother-in-law, Joe, had defined its purpose as aiding delinquent teenage boys. After a number of years of operations, the board of Joe's Home for Delinquent Boys determined that the organization should also expand to offer the same services to teenage girls and preteens as well. If the organization had defined its purposes as aiding delinquent children, then it would be able to immediately expand its operations. Because of its narrow purpose clause, the board is now faced with having to amend the articles to expand the purpose. Further, the board will have to determine whether its assets can be used for these expansion efforts, or whether they must be used for the more limited purpose initially indicated (see Part II, Raising and Spending Money, Designated Gifts).

The purpose should also be consistent with the exempt status desired. For example, if the organization expects to be exempt as a charitable organization so that donations will be deductible as charitable contributions, the purpose, as set forth in the Articles of Incorporation, must fit under the charitable types of purposes listed in section 501(c)(3) of the Internal Revenue Code. In other words, it must be organized "exclusively for religious, charitable, scientific, testing for public safety, literary or educational purposes or for the prevention of cruelty to children or animals." If the purpose clause does not fit into one of these categories, it will not be tax-exempt under section 501(c)(3).

Agent for Service of Process

By law, each corporation is a person separate from any individual involved. As it has no corporal body, someone must be designated to accept service of process in the event the corporation is sued. This person is referred to as the "agent for service of process," or the "corporate agent." The agent may be either an individual or another corporation that has specifically registered to serve in such a capacity, and the agent must be located in the state of incorporation. Since Sam has decided to incorporate in his own state, he may serve as the agent himself. If he had decided to incorporate in another state, he might have had to pay a corporation in that state to serve as agent for service of process on behalf of his new corporation.

Whoever is chosen to serve as the agent must be reliable. If an agent is served and does not take steps to make sure the lawsuit is answered appropriately, a default judgment may be entered against the corporation.

If a person not involved in the actual operations is chosen, the organization will need to keep the person informed. For example, Sam might ask Alvin to serve as the agent, knowing that Alvin is reliable. But if Sam and Save the Chipmunks subsequently move without letting Alvin know the new address and telephone number, it will be difficult for Alvin to notify Save the Chipmunks of service and any delay might again result in a default judgment being entered against the corporation.

Required Provisions for 501(c)(3) Status

There are several provisions required if the organization is to establish its exempt status under section 501(c)(3) of the Internal Revenue Code. These provisions limit the activities of the organization to those permitted by 501(c)(3) organizations, and provide that all assets will be used for the exempt purpose of the organization. A dissolution clause must also be included, specifying what organization or organizations, or types of organizations if no specific organization is named, will receive the assets in the event of dissolution.

Other State-specific Provisions

Some states require additional provisions. For example, some require that all of the initial directors be named (and sometimes their addresses), and may require that each initial director sign the articles.

Another provision sometimes required is whether or not the organization's existence is perpetual. A term of years is not recommended. XYZ Christian Church had provided for a 50-year existence, but no one bothered to make a note of this. Fortunately, some 75 years after its incorporation, someone noted that the term had expired, and amended Articles were filed after the fact.

Some states require that the articles be published after being filed with the Secretary of State.

Alvin should review his state law to make sure that every required provision is included in Sam's Articles.

Some state provisions are not obvious. For example, in California certain types of property tax exemptions require specific language in the Articles before the exemption will be available.

Optional Provisions

Although provisions that are normally in the bylaws may also be in the Articles, Sam should consider including only necessary provisions in the Articles to avoid conflicts between the documents. Bylaws are more easily amended as the organization grows and needs change.

There are other optional provisions that should be included. For example, some states allow for limited liability of the directors, but require that this limitation be set forth in the Articles. And if the organization is to be under the control of another entity, this fact may also have to be set forth in the Articles to be fully effective.

Filing

When filing the Articles with the Secretary of State or other designated governmental agency, it is good to include an extra copy or two of the Articles to be certified and returned. This allows the corporation to keep one clean copy in its corporate minute book and to use the other as a "working copy" for when copies are needed to open bank accounts, etc. A nominal fee may be charged for the extra copy, but it is worth the money to get it.

Noncorporate Entities

With a trust or an unincorporated association, there are no documents that need to be filed to begin the existence of the organization. There will generally be a trust document or articles of association that set forth many of the same provisions as would be in the Articles and/or bylaws of a corporation.

An LLC will have to file Articles of Organization or a similar document with the state to begin its existence. An LLC should also have an operating agreement to avoid statutory default provisions. This is especially important for a nonprofit entity, as the statutory default provisions are generally geared to business entities.

Any nonprofit entity that plans to be tax exempt will have to include the appropriate provisions in its organizational documents.

Summary of First Step: Articles of Incorporation

Articles must include	Name of corporation
	Purpose clause
	Name and address for agent for service of process
	If charitable, provisions dedicating assets to charitable purpose
	If charitable, provisions requiring distribution of assets to other exempt organizations upon dissolution
	Other provisions required by state law
Articles may include	Names and addresses of initial directors
	If allowed, provisions limiting liability of directors
	Other provisions for governing organization (generally included in bylaws rather than articles)
Sign and date	If directors listed, may need to be signed by all directors; generally only need signature of incorporator. Check law.
File (along with required filing fee)	With Secretary of State or other designated state agency. Include extra copies to be certified.
Publish	Some states require publication of articles and amendments.

SECOND STEP: Determine How the Corporation Will Be Governed

Bylaws

As noted above, the bylaws are a set of internal rules by which the nonprofit operates. They define how it functions, such as qualifications for the corporation's directors and members (if any), rules for noticing and conducting meetings, rules for electing and removing directors, rules for disciplining members and/or suspending membership rights, a description of the role and responsibilities of committees, a description of the duties of corporate officers, and other similar information. While these are not filed with the Secretary of State's office, they must be submitted to taxing authorities as part of an application for exempt status and generally have the force of law within the organization.

Well-drafted bylaws need to be rather complex. If a particular item is not addressed in the Articles or the bylaws, the rule that will be applied is the default provision contained in the law of the state of incorporation. This may not be the result desired. Further, even if the default rules are satisfactory, most people do not have a copy of their state laws readily available. Setting forth the desired rules in the bylaws allows everyone to know how the organization is to be operated.

What I would *not* put in the bylaws is a requirement that the corporation follow *Robert's Rules of Order*. First, these rules sometimes conflict with state law. Secondly, they are overly complex for most nonprofit organizations. Finally, the vast majority of people do not understand these rules, resulting in the need for a parliamentarian, and concentrating the power in the hands of a few who know how to manipulate the rules and who may prevent others from having any significant input in decisions reached.

Organizations sometimes choose to have a constitution instead of or in addition to the bylaws (for some reason, religious organizations often do this). There is no need to have two such documents, and in fact this can cause problems if they are contradictory. The two should be merged unless there is a way of clearly defining what is in one and what is in the other so that there is no overlap.

"Well," says Sam, "what information do I need to give to you, so that you can draft bylaws for me? What decisions do I need to make?"

General Structure: What Hat Are You Wearing?

The first thing Sam needs to do is understand the different types of hats people involved with the organization may wear. The following is a simple guideline to help Sam decide what he wants when drafting bylaws for his corporation. A person may wear different hats; however he or she must know what hat he or she is wearing when taking a particular action.

Members elect directors and generally vote on major decisions, such as mergers and dissolutions. Members in nonprofit corporations are similar to shareholders in business corporations. The rights of members may be modified by the bylaws. Many nonprofits do not have members.

Directors direct. They make policy decisions for the corporation and decide on its overall direction. Directors act as a body; they have no power to act alone (thus the "board" of directors).

Officers implement. The directors normally elect officers; the directors may elect themselves or others to serve as officers. The officers carry out the responsibilities delegated to them by the directors or assigned by the bylaws, and they report back to the directors.

Directors sometimes form **committees**. In some states, a committee with board powers (a "board committee") must be made up of only directors. Committees are formed for a specific task that can be ongoing or designed to accomplish a particular task.

All actions taken by the members, directors, and committees on behalf of the corporation must be documented in the corporate minutes.

Members

"So should my corporation have members?" Sam asks.

There are two basic situations where nonprofits have members. In the first situation, a number of individuals have an ongoing interest in the management of the nonprofit. For example, a congregational church will generally have a membership made up of those in the congregation over a certain age who adhere to its religious beliefs and have joined as members. The number of members is normally substantially in excess of the number of directors; they choose the directors to make the decisions on their behalf.

The second situation involves a limited number of members. For example, with a nonprofit organization that is funded almost wholly by a particular individual, that individual may want to have others serve as directors, yet may want to retain the ability to elect future directors personally. This can be done by having a limited membership (perhaps the individual and his or her spouse), but a larger board. To avoid potential conflicts, it is recommended that this structure be used only when the individual and his or her relatives do not benefit from the corporation (either as employees or beneficiaries).

Many nonprofits have determined that there is no need for members. In such a situation, the directors become self-perpetuating; i.e., they elect themselves or others as directors. Alternatively, the bylaws may provide another method of choosing directors, such as having some or all appointed by related organizations (who may or may not be considered members), having some serve automatically by virtue of another position, or having the directors elected by delegates.

Members of a nonprofit corporation function similarly to shareholders, although they are not owners and are not issued stock. Mutual benefit corporations, such as homeowners associations and social clubs, may be an exception to this rule, as they may actually have an ownership interest in the corporation.

Members generally vote for directors and on major issues facing the organization, such as whether to merge or dissolve the corporation or to sell all or substantially all of its assets. They do not have any power over the actual operations of the organization, and generally they do not have the accompanying liability.[7]

A problem many nonprofit organizations have with members is keeping track of them. Because they have authority over the organization and voting rights, it is important to keep an up-to-date membership list. Unfortunately, because the members of most nonprofit organizations, including all charitable organizations exempt under 501(c)(3) of the Internal Revenue Code, have no ownership interest or property rights in the organization, members may move or otherwise cease their involvement with the organization without letting the organization know. Because of this, if the corporation has members, it must make sure it has a regular method for verifying membership and removing members when they cease to be active, or no longer have contact with the organization. This can be done any number of ways, such as by requiring the payment of annual membership dues, by requiring an annual verification that the individual wishes to continue to be a member, or by requiring that the members attend a certain number of functions annually to maintain their membership in good standing. Whatever method the organization

---

7. If the members reserve certain powers to themselves, then the issue arises as to whether they will be liable as directors would be if they exercise these powers.

chooses to use, it should make sure that the membership list is updated on a regular basis—at least once a year. Shortly before the annual meeting would be the most appropriate time to update these records.

A corporation generally cannot alter provisions concerning members (if it has them) without the members' approval. So it is reasonable to consider at the time of formation if the organization should have members. It is much harder to take rights away from members than it is not to give them any rights in the first place.

"It sounds to me like I probably don't want members," Sam muses. "I don't want to have to track down people to get their votes."

But then he remembers that the Museum of Art has members and collects dues each year from the members. "I've been a member for the last five years," he continues, "and they have never let me choose the directors. Are they doing something wrong? Or can I have members and charge them dues without giving them the right to vote?

Many corporations choose to use the term "members" as a fund-raising device, rather than for corporate governance. In these situations (such as with the art institute Sam has joined), a member has no authority and no right to vote. This is generally permissible and, in fact, is expressly permitted by most state laws. However, the organization should specifically define the term "member" in the bylaws and, if "member" is going to be only a fund-raising term, it should be so limited. If it is not, then anyone called a member may have the rights and duties described in the state statute.

If a corporation chooses to have members, the bylaws should set forth how one becomes a member, how a member is removed, the requirements for holding meetings, and any powers that are reserved to the members. This will include the percentage of members necessary to have a meeting (a "quorum") and the percentage of votes necessary to take action (generally a majority of a quorum, unless a higher percentage is required by the bylaws or state law).

Note that if the organization is a trust, it will not have members (although it may have beneficiaries). An unincorporated association will have members, as will a limited liability company (although, as noted above, to date the IRS has found LLCs to be exempt only if their members are also exempt).

Who Is a Director?

"Okay, I will think about maybe having 'members' to raise funds, but make sure you don't give them the right to vote when you draft my Bylaws," says Sam. "We shouldn't have any problems with control, since I thought I would just elect myself, my wife, and my brother as directors, and we would be ready to go. Won't that work?"

Well, maybe and maybe not.

Let's talk first about what Directors do.

- Directors have no individual authority; they must act jointly as a board.
- Directors make the basic policy decisions for the corporation.

Because it is essential to the organization's tax exempt status that it abide by its stated purposes, one of the principal duties of a director is to be aware of the nature and extent of the nonprofit's exempt purposes and to assure that those purposes are properly pursued. **The purpose of every act and decision of a director should be to advance the nonprofit's purpose.** If the personal aims of the individual are not the same as the aims of the organization, then the individual should not serve as a director. In no event should a director initiate or knowingly support or allow actions that will either exceed or defeat the nonprofit's stated purpose.

Put another way, each decision should be made based on what is best for the organization. The IRS and many states' Attorneys General want to make sure that the board can do this. There is a concern that if the board is made up of related individuals, it is possible that the corporation may be run in a manner that benefits these individuals, rather than all of the assets being used to advance the purpose. Therefore, it is recommended that a majority of the board be unrelated.

"Well," says Sam, "when you say that you would *recommend* that a majority of directors be unrelated, is this an actual requirement?"

"It depends, Sam, on whether you or any of your relatives are going to be compensated. The laws of your state provide that a majority of your directors must be uncompensated and not related to anyone who is compensated.[8] Are you going to serve as the executive director of the corporation? And if so, will you want to be paid for your services?"

Sam probably is going to be the executive director or president of the corporation, at least initially, but does not know if he will receive any type of compensation, partly because he does not know what type of support the organization may generate. But because he might want compensation at some point in the future, he might want to set up a more diverse board.

The other issue with having related board members, especially with a public charity, is the concern of the IRS that the organization be operated exclusively for charitable purposes. In order to make it more likely that there is no impermissible benefit, the IRS may demand that the organization have a majority of directors who are unrelated to each other before it grants the organization a tax-exempt status.

In any event, Sam will want to have the board adopt a conflict of interest policy that will address transactions between the corporation and any officers or directors or their relatives. Refer to Part II, Enforcement of Laws, Conflicts of Interest, and Appendix A.

How Many Directors Should Be on the Board?

"Well, if I am not going to be employed by the organization, maybe I should just be the sole director, like I am for my business corporation," said Sam. "That way I can control the organization and not worry about conflicts of interest and disputes among directors. Can I do that?"

Not all nonprofits have boards of directors. If the organization is a trust, it will have one or more trustees. And if it is an unincorporated association, it can be operated in any manner seen fit by the members and still be exempt, providing it

---

8. See, e.g., Revised Model Nonprofit Corporation Act, Section 8.13 (1985), which provides that no more than 49% of the directors of a public benefit corporation may be financially interested.

is both organized and operated for exempt purposes. However, if the organization is a corporation, it will have a board.

As to whether or not one individual can constitute the board, the answer is maybe. First of all, the state law under which the organization is created must permit it. For example, in many states, there is a special type of religious organization called a "corporation sole" which is directed by the principal religious leader. If the organization is a corporation sole (such as the Catholic Church, where the bishop functions as the sole director over an area), then one individual does constitute the entire board. If the corporation is a private foundation, then again it may be possible (although perhaps unwise) to have only one director. The organization will have the same challenge as with related directors, of convincing the IRS that the organization has enough checks and balances to assure that will be operated exclusively for charitable purposes.

Generally, the number of directors will vary depending upon the complexity of the organization and the various constituents being represented. With a large, complex medical organization, in order to assure adequate oversight, a larger board may be needed, whereas with a start-up organization like Sam's that has a relatively narrowly defined purpose, a smaller board may be preferable. However, even with a start-up organization, if there are defined constituencies that want representation, the organization may find that a larger board to be helpful. Keep in mind that the larger the board, the harder it will be to have meetings with everyone in attendance. Further, with a large board, an individual director may forget how important it is that he or she continues to fulfill his or her responsibilities to the organization, thinking that others will do the job.

How Many Boards of Directors Should an Organization Have?

"When you talk about a large board, it seems like maybe a better solution is to split the board into more than one board. Sometimes there is so much to do with a nonprofit that having several boards would work better, with each board responsible for a different area. Maybe we could have one board for fund-raising, and another to manage the administration."

"Sam, that is not a good idea," replies Alvin. "Apart from the fact that your organization is too small to have a complex corporate structure, you need someone who is in charge. If you start splitting the board up, it may be that either no one takes responsibility, or the boards end up at odds with each other."

"Does that mean that our new church pastor is right? Pastor Ray doesn't think that a divided board is permissible. Our church bylaws provide for a board of elders, a board of deacons, *and* a board of directors. Each of these boards are delegated certain powers. So far it has worked fine, with the elders handling the spiritual matters, the deacons handling the temporal matters, and the directors handling the paperwork."

"It sounds like you hired a smart man, Sam. However, not only is there a question of who is in charge, but there is another issue: if there is a conflict, which board wins?"

"Alvin, are you sure Pastor Ray hasn't already talked to you? He said the same thing to us. He said that although he liked the church and really liked the congregation, we would have to redo our governance structure if he was going to pastor us. So what should we do?"

One step, of course, is to eliminate duplicate boards. After some discussion, Alvin discovered that the Oak Street Church thought they legally had to have a board of directors to be the "official board," rather than recognizing that the "official board" is the board that has the ultimate authority, regardless of its name. Once this became clear, they quickly decided to eliminate the Board of Directors.

The church continued to want both elders and deacons, as they found both positions to be scriptural, with the elders supervising the spiritual life, and the deacons, the temporal or physical life of the church. Alvin agreed they could continue to have both positions defined, but emphasized that they needed to clarify which board is in charge, with the other board reporting to it about those duties that were specifically under its supervision (like an administrative committee that is delegated certain responsibilities, but has no authority beyond those specifically-delegated responsibilities).

It is true that sometimes a corporation might function better if it does not do everything itself. For example, a board may be spectacularly successful in operations, but not as successful in fund-raising. What some organizations have chosen to do (which generally works better than trying to split the powers of a single entity) is to form a separate corporation for the fund-raising efforts (this entity would normally be a supporting organization for tax purposes). The supporting entity, XYZ Foundation, is able to concentrate on obtaining additional financial support for XYZ Corporation, without interfering with the operational aspects of XYZ Corporation. XYZ Foundation needs to have certain ties with XYZ Corporation. For example, it may have some overlapping directors, or XYZ Corporation board may elect or ratify the election of some or all of the directors of XYZ Foundation, etc. But the Foundation board would include individuals able to contribute or to provide contacts to other potential contributors, rather than being populated with organizational people.

Representing Nonprofits; Serving on the Board

"Since I should probably have some non-family members on the board, and I should probably have more than just me on the board, will you be a director?" Sam asks. "That way I know I will continue to get good legal advice for the corporation."

"Sam," Alvin replies, "I am extremely flattered that you would want me to be a part of your new venture, and I like the concept of what you are doing. But I will have to think about it before giving you an answer."

Should Alvin agree to be part of the board?

Representing a nonprofit corporation and serving on the board of the same nonprofit raises major concerns over conflicts of interest that might arise. The advice Alvin gives as a director and the advice Alvin might give as a lawyer may well be different. If he decides to try to wear both hats at the same time, he must be extremely careful to separate the two. Because he is a lawyer, it is likely that the other directors will look to Alvin for legal advice, even if they do not specifically express this expectation. Alvin should make it clear that he is not giving legal advice unless he is specifically retained for this purpose (whether or not he is paid for the advice).

Another point that Alvin may have realized by now is that the law affecting nonprofits is not simple. Unless he feels comfortable giving advice in a certain area or unless he is willing to spend the time getting up to speed, Alvin may well be better off telling the organization to hire a specialist. Alvin might decide that he would be willing to serve on the board if the corporation hires another attorney to provide legal advice, when necessary. Having said that, many attorneys feel a compulsion to provide legal assistance to their favorite charity, while also serving on the board.

If Alvin were to serve on the board, he should also realize that his professional malpractice insurance will probably not cover this service.

It is also true that whenever anyone is on a board of directors, they cannot ignore their background. Therefore, when a Certified Public Accountant (CPA) serves on the board, clearly he or she is likely to have a better understanding of numbers than someone who is, for example, an artist. The CPA cannot pretend not to be a CPA, but will be held to the reasonable person standard for someone with that same background. Of course, the CPA clearly cannot perform the audit for the organization for which he or she serves as a director (the auditor must always be disinterested). Further, if the CPA spends his or her time doing tax returns for individuals and is not an expert in a particular type of accounting, e.g., cost accounting for manufacturers, the CPA will not be held to the same standard as an expert in that field. The same analogy can be made for attorneys. If an attorney is a specialist in criminal law and never looks at a corporation, the attorney does not have to become an expert in corporate law to serve on a board. However, the attorney should make it clear to the rest of the board what role he or she is playing, so that the rest of the board does not assume that a statement made by the attorney/director is legal advice when, in fact, it is not. The difference, of course, between an attorney and a CPA is that while a CPA performing an audit is required to be disinterested so as to be able to present an unbiased financial statement, attorneys, by nature of their representation of one side, are clearly biased. But if Alvin is wearing his attorney hat during Board discussions, can he function adequately as a director?

It is extremely important to note that there are other significant issues that should be considered before this decision is made. For example, as both a lawyer for the corporation and a director, Alvin might find himself in a place where he is a material witness to the activity of the corporation. In such a situation his legal advice may not be protected by the attorney-client privilege; he might be called to testify as a director; and/or he might be disqualified from representing the organization.

With these issues in mind, it is ultimately Alvin's decision as to whether or not there are too many potential conflicts that come from representing the organization while serving on the board.

Advisory Board

"If you won't be on the board, could I put you on an advisory board?" asks Sam. "Or are you going to tell me that you don't want me to have an advisory board, either?"

Some nonprofits have advisors or an advisory board made up of individuals who have something to offer the organization (like name recognition, specific skills, or money) but who are not in a position to dedicate the time necessary to fulfill the duties of a director. This is essentially an honorary position (unless the bylaws give them some actual power, which is not being recommended and may be prohibited by state law) and allows the organization to receive the benefit of being associated with these individuals. The individuals also get the recognition they desire (and may deserve) without the liability and time commitment of being on the board.

Having an advisory board may also give the organization a place to put former board members who still want to be involved in some way. Sometimes corporations use advisory boards to provide input on specific issues, which can include providing expertise that the board itself does not have.

To make sure that the potential director liability does not extend to the advisory board, it must be clear that the advisors have no responsibility other than to advise, and that they have no power to require that their advice be followed.

Are You an Officer or a Director?

"Okay," says Sam. "Maybe you can make a provision that I can have an advisory board later. But for now, I will have three directors: I will be the president, Bill will be the secretary, and Susan will be the treasurer."

"Wait a minute, Sam. You are making the common mistake of confusing directors with officers. Although an individual may be both a director and an officer, they are distinct positions. While the directors may elect themselves as officers, they may decide that someone not a director would be better in a certain position. I can draft the paperwork for you with the three of you being both the directors and the officers, but you need to understand that these are different hats."

"Well, but isn't the Executive Director a director?" asks Sam.

"No. Someone who has 'director' in their title, such as an 'executive director,' a 'program director,' or a 'director of development' is not automatically on the board. Unless the executive director is elected to the board as a director, or unless the bylaws automatically appoint the executive director to the board, then that person is not serving on the board. Generally this would be clear, as the directors are normally elected positions. However, if there is confusion, either the executive director, program director, director of development, or the directors serving on the board may be referred to by some other name (a church, for example, might choose to have its board referred to as a Board of Elders)."

What are the differences between a director and an officer?

Directors direct. They set policy and make major decisions. They are the ultimate authority for the organization. They operate jointly, as a Board of Directors, rather than separately.

The directors generally elect officers. The officers are responsible for the day-to-day activities of the organization and for implementing the decisions of the board. Unlike directors, who can only act jointly, officers act individually. However, officers are authorized to carry out only the responsibilities that have been delegated to them by the directors, and they must report back to the directors as to how the corporation is progressing in meeting its goals.

An individual may be both an officer and a director if elected to serve in both positions; however, the individual must make sure what hat is being worn at any given time. As an officer, the individual implements the activities approved by the Board of Directors and reports to the Board of Directors. As a director, the individual, collectively with the rest of the board, supervises the entire operation of the corporation.

The officers that a corporation often has are: a chief executive officer (generally called a president, sometimes an executive director), a secretary, and a treasurer. Some state corporation laws allow for whatever officers the corporation wants; some may require additional officers (such as a vice president). The corporation may have a Chair of the Board (either instead of or in addition to the president).

In a large organization, the Chair of the Board, who runs the board meetings, is generally a director as well as an officer. The president or executive director may be a paid staff position, responsible for the actual operations of the corporation, and not a director. The secretary is responsible for records such as the minutes and the membership roster. The treasurer oversees the finances, generally under the oversight of both the president and the board.

Some organizations choose to split the treasurer position into board officer and staff officer positions. The treasurer may be a director with oversight responsibilities. The chief financial officer would then be the staff person in charge of the actual day-to-day accounting functions.

Normally the president or CEO reports directly to the board. Officers other than "board officers" (e.g., the Chair and perhaps the Treasurer) report to the president.

Both board officers and staff officers have individual duties and responsibilities, and they act independently when carrying out their "officer" duties. When the officer positions are split like this, the board officers are generally uncompensated, where the staff officers are often employees.

"If the officers are not the same as the directors, should Bill still be the secretary, or should I actually choose someone with secretarial skills to fill this position?"

If Bill, who is to be the secretary, cannot type, another staff member can actually take the notes, send out the notices, etc., under the direction of the secretary. But being the corporate secretary is more than taking notes. He or she must be a person that the board finds to be competent and trustworthy. The secretary is often the person who signs on behalf of the organization. Thus, you will want someone in this position who has a good grasp of what is going on and will not sign something that has not been authorized by the board.

"I think I will keep Bill as the Secretary," muses Sam.

Employees Serving as Directors

"I have another question. If Save The Chipmunks really takes off and I can work as a full-time CEO, will there be any problem if I continue to be a voting member of the board? My brother told me that I couldn't work for the organization and still be on the board."

"Well, Sam, as with many of your questions, the answer is, 'Maybe.'"

Some people take the position that it is never a good idea, and they will sometimes actually provide in the bylaws that directors cannot be employees.

However, you clearly want and need an interested board of directors, especially with small start-up nonprofits. Sometimes the only way to assure that the organization gets off the ground is to make sure that the person with the vision also is involved in the policy/decision making process of the board. On the other hand, if the CEO is on the board, the board must take extra steps to make sure it has all of the needed information, and is not simply rubber-stamping the decisions of the CEO. Of course, this can happen even if the CEO is not on the board, if you have a strong CEO and a deferential board. The solution is to make sure that everyone on the board understands their responsibilities and duties and carries them out.

What does NOT work is to have a situation where the CEO is not on the board, but one or more of the CEO's staff are directors. This puts the CEO in the untenable position of reporting to his or her own staff, while at the same time being responsible to oversee their work. No one should be required to report to a subordinate.

In any event, the CEO should not be involved in either setting his or her compensation or evaluation. It can be done either by a personnel committee, or by the rest of the board, apart from the CEO. If the CEO is an employee of the organization and a member of the Board, I would recommend that there be a separate Board Chair who runs the meetings and is responsible for obtaining the evaluation(s) of the CEO.

Committees

To be more effective, directors sometimes form committees to which they delegate certain duties. This can be especially helpful when the corporation has a large board and many responsibilities. In a number of states, members of a committee with board powers (a "board committee") must be made up of directors. In these states, a committee with non-directors is an administrative committee that, like officers, may implement only such responsibilities as are specifically delegated by the directors; they cannot make board-level decisions.

The board may appoint committees for almost any purpose. Most states do not allow a committee to exercise certain powers, such as the right to vote for directors, to amend the articles, approve merger agreements, etc. These powers may only be exercised by the full board.

If a committee is appointed by the Board to accomplish a single specific task with the view that the committee will dissolve upon completion of that task, it is generally termed a "special committee." If a committee is established to perform an ongoing function on behalf of the corporation, the committee is often designated as a "standing committee."

The following committees are typical standing committees:

1. Executive Committee. The need for an executive committee depends upon the organization. The basic concept is that the executive committee acts in place of the board, in between board meetings. If the board is small and all the directors are located in the same general vicinity, it is generally easy to get the entire board together for special meetings. However, if it is large and located across the United States, a special meeting is likely to be much more difficult to hold. If an emergency situation arises that needs immediate board action, it has been found to be beneficial to have a small executive committee with the power to act for the board.

Unfortunately, some organizations have used the executive committee as a "super board" to limit what the entire board can consider, by requiring all items to first go to the executive committee before they can be brought up before the full board. Allowing a limited number of directors to usurp the powers of the board is not an appropriate use of the executive committee. It should always be remembered that the executive committee reports to the board, and not the other way around. Because of this, and because of the increased ability to communicate through such means as conference telephones and electronically, there has been a move away from using executive committees.

2. Governance Committee. This committee is responsible to assure the correct functioning of the board. It often is responsible for board education, for making sure each director knows and is fulfilling his or her duties, and for locating qualified candidates with the backgrounds needed to effectively "round out" the board. It is sometimes responsible to nominate candidates for other positions, such as the officers. The governance committee should be made up of directors who are free of relationships that would interfere with their exercise of independent judgment in the selection of qualified nominees as directors or principal officers. Both the fact and appearance of objectivity are important. To avoid the appearance of control by an inside group, the members of this committee might be rotated on a regular basis.

3. Finance Committee. This committee supervises the preparation of budgets and regularly reviews financial materials. It should be comprised of directors who are familiar with financial matters. This is sometimes combined with the audit committee. However, under new rules now being adopted by some states to increase accountability of nonprofits, it may need to be a separate committee.

4. Audit Committee. This committee should be comprised of directors who are able to make informed decisions concerning matters such as the selection of an auditor, meeting with the auditor concerning any issues the auditor or the board have concerning the financial status of the organization, and review and acceptance of the audit report. The directors on the audit committee should not be involved in operational matters, as this may jeopardize its independence from management.

5. Personnel Committee. A principal responsibility of the board is reviewing the CEO's job performance and setting compensation. Under some new laws, the compensation of the CFO or Treasurer must also be approved by the board. These responsibilities are sometimes delegated to a Personnel or Compensation Committee. All salaries paid by a nonprofit must be reasonable, particularly when they are paid to persons who are in a position to exercise substantial influence over the organization; by definition this includes both the CEO and the CFO (Refer to Part II, Enforcement of Laws, "Intermediate Sanctions"). Reasonableness should be determined by reference to outside objective facts, such as a salary survey.

In Sam's case, he does not have a large board (only three directors). Therefore, it is unlikely that he will make much use of board committees, although he might form an "administrative committee" with nonboard members to help with specific projects, such as putting on a fund-raising event. Alvin will allow for committees in the bylaws, but will not require any specific standing committees.

Summary of Second Step: Determine How Corporation Will Be Governed

If directors are not listed in articles	Select directors
Select officers	Some states require specific officers
Draft bylaws	Include name and location of organization
	Purpose (optional: If included, make same as purpose in articles)
	Whether or not to have members
If corporation has members	How members are chosen and removed
	Provisions to call and hold meetings, when annual meeting will be, quorum requirements, etc.
	What are members rights (e.g., elect directors, vote on amendments to articles, bylaws, changes such as mergers, dissolutions)
Directors	How and when directors are chosen, what are their terms, how can they be removed
	How many directors
	Duties of directors
	Provisions to call and hold meetings of directors, quorum requirements, etc.
Committees	Committee structure
	If desired, description of standing committees
	If desired, authorize nonboard committees
Officers	What officers the corporation will have
	How officers are chosen (normally by directors; however staff officers may be chosen by CEO)
	Responsibilities of each officer
Other provisions	Indemnification provisions
	How bylaws are amended
	Other provisions desired
	Dissolution provisions (optional). Note: these must not conflict with dissolution provisions in articles

THIRD STEP: Electing Directors, Initial Meeting, and Subsequent Meetings

Prior to actually setting up his corporation, Sam may have whatever organizational meetings he desires.

The corporation begins its existence upon the filing of the Articles. Once the Articles are filed, unless the initial directors are listed in the Articles, the incorporator may take whatever actions he or she deems are necessary. Generally, the incorporator fulfills his or her duties simply by electing the directors, and sometimes by adopting the bylaws.

At that point, the directors take over. The initial directors (either those listed in the Articles or elected by the incorporator) should have their first "organizational" meeting. At this meeting, the directors will authorize such actions as are necessary to complete the organization of the corporation, such as adopting bylaws (if not done by the incorporator), electing officers, opening bank accounts, and such other matters as are necessary to begin operations.

Observance of Corporate Formalities

The corporation is considered to be a "person" apart from any of the individuals that are a part of the corporation.

In order to make it clear that an action taken on behalf of the corporation is actually an act of the corporation, and not just an act of the individuals involved with the corporation, it is necessary that the decisions made and the actions taken be documented as being done by or on behalf of the corporation. To do this, the corporation must function according to the requirements set forth in the law and the bylaws. Otherwise, someone may be able to claim that a particular action was the act of the individual or individuals. If this happens, the individuals may be found to be personally liable when they thought they were acting on behalf of the entity.

For example, directors generally take action, either by having a meeting that is attended by a quorum, or by having all of the directors sign a resolution agreeing to take the action. Minutes of each meeting are necessary to document what actions the board approved, and are thus actions of the corporation.

How Many Meetings?

"So how often does the board have to meet?" asks Sam. "Can we meet once a year, or must meetings be held more often to meet legal requirements?"

The corporation's board should meet as often as is necessary to accomplish the mission of the organization. Many organizations have directors meetings three times a year; others have meetings each month (required by some funding sources); others find one meeting a year to be sufficient.

Sam may wish to provide for one regular annual meeting a year in his bylaws, treating other meetings as special meetings. That way, if the board normally meets monthly but decides to cancel the December meeting, it will not be in violation of its bylaws as it would be if monthly meetings were required.

The date, time, and place of regular meetings are normally specified in the bylaws. Notice need not be given if the meeting is held as specified.

Notice of the time, date, and place (and sometimes what will be discussed) of all special meetings, or regular meetings held at a different time, date, or location must be given to the directors in accordance with the provisions of state law and the bylaws.

If notice is not given, the meeting can still be held, as long as the directors not attending sign a Waiver of Notice.

Action by the Board and Attendance at Meetings

"What if everyone can't get together at the same time? Can we still take action?"

There are two ways that the board can authorize an action.

One way is to have all of the directors sign and date a resolution (a "unanimous written consent").[9] If this is done, a meeting does not even have to be held. The action will be effective upon the last signature.

The second way is to have a meeting. The bylaws will set forth the number of people who must be present before action may be taken (a "quorum"). A quorum is normally a majority, although for some actions, a larger number may be required, either by the bylaws or by state law. In Sam's case, because he will have a three-member board, there must be at least two present before the board can act.

"Can I hold my board meetings by using an Internet chatroom instead of a face-to-face setting? Bill lives in another city and would incur travel expenses if he has to actually attend each meeting."

Although the particulars may vary by state, meetings can normally be held in any fashion that allows all of the members to communicate with each other. A telephone conference call is the common method; electronic communication, as long as it is done in a manner where everyone is communicating *at the same time*, will generally also comply with the law. What is probably *not* currently permitted is to have an ongoing message board, where people come and go, leaving messages for each other over a period of days or weeks. Although this is a way that an issue can be fully discussed, at some point there needs to be a "meeting" where the matter is put to a vote and a decision is made.

"Well," says Sam, "that reminds me of another question: Is it legal to consult with directors on a one-to-one basis in-between board meetings? We would like to look to our directors for input when situations arise in which their expertise would be important. For example, Susan is a renowned environmentalist, and she may be able to provide specific input on how to make the environment more chipmunk friendly."

The type of consultation Sam is suggesting is perfectly acceptable, but he needs to understand that this is not making use of Susan as a director, but rather in her professional capacity. As we noted before, directors, as such, may not operate individually, but are only able to act as directors collectively.

"Do I have to allow anyone to attend a meeting? Someone told me that there was an "Open Meeting" law and that if I got money from the government, I would have to open the board meetings to nondirectors."

Open meeting laws are creations of the state. Therefore, it depends on your state law. For example, in California, unless you are a governmental entity, you do not need to make your meetings open to the public, even if you receive funding from the government.

"What if I want someone else to attend the board meeting?"

An organization may often have management staff attend and participate in a board meeting. If the management staff is meeting with the board, then it is a board meeting, and the staff is simply attending at the pleasure of the board. The board

---

9. Some states allow less than unanimous written consent.

may choose to invite specific people to attend the meetings, or it may open the meetings for others to attend, as it sees fit. However, just because management staff or others may attend, they have no vote on board matters unless they are elected to the board.

Summary of Third Step: Electing Directors; Initial and Subsequent Meetings

If directors are not specified in articles:	Incorporator elects directors
	Prior to election of directors, Incorporator may take other actions that would otherwise be taken by directors
Directors hold initial meeting	Actions taken should include:
	• Adopt bylaws
	• Elect Officers
	• Authorize bank accounts/signatories on accounts
	• Authorize filings to establish exempt status
	• Authorize payment of incorporation expenses, ratify pre-incorporation actions
	• Choose accounting year
	• Establish principal place of business
	• Select new agent for service of process, if desired
	• Authorize continuing filing of necessary governmental forms
	• Authorize such other matters as are necessary to begin operations
	• Adopt conflict of interest policy
Approval of additional items	There are two methods to approve items after the initial meeting:
	• Send out notice of meeting or have directors sign a waiver of notice, and hold meeting at time, date, and place specified (meeting must be attended by quorum of directors)
	• Have a Unanimous Written Consent signed by all directors, approving action to be taken (Majority Written Consent in some states)

FOURTH STEP: Establish Exempt Status

Types of Exemptions

"As soon as I file my articles of incorporation, will I be able to start raising funds and operating the entity?"

"Not so fast, Sam. The organization will be in existence, and you will be able to begin operations. However, as we already discussed, nonprofit does not mean tax-exempt. Nonprofit means it has been formed/incorporated as a nonprofit, generally under the state nonprofit corporation act. But to be tax exempt, you need to fit under one of the code sections that defines the different types of nonprofits. If you want to be exempt under section 501(c)(3) of the Internal Revenue Service, you must file with the IRS to establish your exempt status. You may also need to file separately with your state taxing authority."

"I need to have the IRS make a determination of my exempt status before I qualify?"

"If you want to be exempt under section 501(c)(3). For any of the other types of nonprofits, you may, but are not required, to establish your exempt status with the IRS."

"I don't think my church has ever filed with the IRS. I asked them last year for a copy of their IRS letter, and they said they did not have one. Does that mean that the contributions I gave to them are not deductible?"

"Your contribution deduction to your church is still okay, Sam. Although most organizations must establish their exempt status with the IRS before they will be considered as 501(c)(3) exempt organizations, there are exceptions to this filing requirement. Churches[10] and organizations with annual gross income of less than $5000 will automatically be considered to be exempt. The only problem is that if the IRS audits the donor, it will be up to the donor to prove he or she gave to an organization that is exempt under section 501(c)(3)[11]; whereas if the church had established its exempt status, the IRS examiner would look up the organization in the IRS list of exempt organizations,[12] find it listed,[13] and go on to the next item."

"Well then, I still don't understand what good a letter of exemption is. My church does not have one, but my donations are deductible. But even though my chamber of commerce has a letter from the IRS, I was told that I could not deduct my dues as charitable contributions."

"Not all exempt organizations are 501(c)(3) charitable organizations. There are over 25 different types of exempt organizations, most of which are listed in Section 501(c) of the Internal Revenue Code. All of these are exempt from taxation; only Section 501(c)(3) organizations have the benefit of contributions being deductible as charitable contributions."

"Alvin, please slow down. I'm not sure I understand."

"Okay, let me put it this way: If you look at section 501 of the Internal Revenue Code, there are numerous different subsections under which a nonprofit may be tax-exempt. Each type of exempt organization has its own requirements.

For example, a nonprofit school, hospital, church, or museum would normally be exempt under section 501(c)(3) of the Internal Revenue Code. This type of nonprofit, which benefits some significant segment of the general population and not a particular person or persons, is what most people think of when they refer

10. "Church," under the Internal Revenue Code, includes temples, mosques, synagogues, and any other house of worship. It is not limited to a particular religion. Integrated auxiliaries of churches and conventions or associations of churches are also exempt from the filing requirements.

11. Because large contributors are quite often not willing to go through this process, they may insist on seeing an exempt determination letter before they make a contribution.

12. Publication 78, Cumulative List of Organizations described in Section 170(c) of the Internal Revenue Code of 1986. This can be found at http://www.irs.gov/charities/index.html under Search for Charities.

13. Sometimes an organization does not make it into the list or is dropped from the list. If you have an existing organization, it would be appropriate to check the list periodically to make sure your organization is listed. If not, you should contact the IRS to get this corrected.

to a nonprofit or exempt organization. Only contributions to Section 501(c)(3) organizations may be deductible as charitable contributions.[14] I think this is where your organization would fit.

If your organization was charitable, but did not benefit a sufficiently large number of people, it might be exempt under section 501(c)(4) as a social welfare organization.

Agricultural and labor organizations are exempt under section 501(c)(5).

Other organizations, such as your chamber of commerce, business leagues, and professional associations, are exempt from taxation under section 501(c)(6) of the Code. Even under this section, to be exempt, the organization must be open to a broad segment of the market. An IBM Users' Group or a Midas Mufflers Dealers Association would not qualify, as such a narrow focus is thought to benefit IBM or Midas more than the general public. A personal computer user's group, not limited by brand, or a mufflers dealers' association that allowed any muffler dealer to participate might be allowed. Payments to a 501(c)(6) like your chamber of commerce may qualify as a business expense, even though a charitable contribution deduction is not available.

A social club would be exempt under section 501(c)(7). Again there is a limitation: normally the club must obtain most of its income directly from its members. If its facilities are open to the general public, then there is nothing to distinguish it from a business. However, if it may be used by only the members themselves and their guests, then the club will not be taxed on that income. As the members of the club pay for and receive the benefit of these expenditures, there is no charitable contribution and no business expense deduction."

Requirements for Exempt Status under 501(c)(3)

"So what, exactly is a section 501(c)(3) organization? I understand that I want one, and that contributions are deductible. But I'm still a little lost here when you talk about code sections."

"I'm sorry, Sam. I forget that not all people talk in 'code' like tax attorneys do. Let's back up to the beginning."

Basic requirements. Section 501(c)(3) of the Internal Revenue Code defines a tax-exempt charitable organization to be:

" ... organized and operated exclusively for religious, charitable, scientific, testing for public safety, literary or educational purposes ... or for the prevention of cruelty to children or animals"

What does this mean?

Must have one or more exempt purposes. We already talked about the fact that the purpose of the organization is paramount, and that the organization needs to clearly define this purpose.

This purpose must fit into one of the categories listed, e.g., charitable, educational, religious, scientific, etc.

---

14. The Internal Revenue Code section under which the *organization* is exempt is 501(c)(3); *contributions* to a 501(c)(3) organization are actually deductible under Section 170 of the Internal Revenue Code.

The term "charitable" is very broad. It includes not only relief of the poor and distressed, but also the advancement of education, religion, or science, lessening the burdens of government, and promoting social welfare by activities which lessen neighborhood tensions, eliminate prejudice and discrimination, defend human and civil rights, or combat community deterioration and juvenile delinquency.

Educational activities include the instruction of individuals in order to improve their abilities, and "the instruction of the public on subjects useful to the individual and beneficial to the community."

"Scientific" refers to the conduct of scientific research efforts in the public interest. This will qualify if the results of the research are made available to the public, the research is performed for a government entity, or the research is directed toward benefiting the public.

Must be organized exclusively for exempt purposes. This brings us back to the Articles of Incorporation. The purpose, as set forth in the Articles, must be limited to one or more exempt purposes within the scope of Section 501(c)(3). Although the purpose must be broad enough to permit the organization to meet its goals, the purpose cannot allow the organization to engage, to any substantial degree, in nonexempt purposes.

In practice, the IRS requires charities to include in their Articles language providing that a charity's assets are irrevocably dedicated to one or more exempt purposes. This includes a provision that on dissolution, the assets will be distributed to another exempt organization.

Must be operated exclusively for exempt purposes. In addition to being *organized* for exempt purposes, the organization must actually be *operated* for exempt purposes. The statute uses the word exclusively, but it is sufficient if the organization is operated primarily for exempt purposes—an "insubstantial part" of the activities may have nonexempt purposes. In looking at the operations, the IRS wants to know exactly how the organization plans to carry out its purposes.

If the organization changes either its purposes or its activities, the organization should let the IRS know of the change, so that it may re-evaluate the organization to make sure it continues to qualify for exemption.

No assets may be used to benefit any private person. The code goes on to require that:

"No part of the net earnings of [the organization] inures to the benefit of any private shareholder or individual . . . ."

As has already been mentioned, the assets of the organization must be used for the charitable purpose for which the organization was formed. In fact, if the organization is found to be operating to benefit an individual connected with the organization rather than the purpose, the exempt status of the organization can be revoked.

"Now, wait a minute. Does this mean that I can't pay myself or anyone else who provides services to the organization? How can we operate?"

"Calm down, Sam. Where the benefit to an individual is an unavoidable by-product of actions taken for the organization's exempt purpose, there is no inurement. As long as the payment is to advance the purpose, rather than to benefit the individual, it is permissible. Of course, the payment needs to be reasonable. We will talk about that in a minute."

Lobbying and political activity. Finally, the code provides that:

"No substantial part of the activities of which is carrying on propaganda or otherwise attempting to influence legislation, and which does not attempt to participate or intervene in any political campaign."

"Does this mean that we cannot contact our legislators about improving the habitat for chipmunks? That would really limit our abilities to function."

"No, Sam. There are two parts to this. An exempt organization *may* engage in lobbying as long as it is an insubstantial part of its activities. However, it *cannot* engage in any political activity—which is supporting or opposing a candidate running for public office."

May attempt to influence legislation. Put another way, a charity may engage in legislative lobbying if the lobbying is a small part of its overall activities. Although there is no clear line about what is substantial, most people agree that 5% is probably insubstantial; more may be allowed.

Public charities, other than churches, may avoid being subject to this vague term by electing to be covered by a mechanical test. This election is contained in 501(h) of the Internal Revenue Code. If the organization makes this election, it will be able to follow a sliding scale that clearly indicates the percentage of lobbying expenditures that are permitted.[15]

"So we can talk to our legislators. How about informing our members and having them contact the legislators? I think they often respond better when they hear directly from their constituents."

"Sam, both of these can be done. Contacting your members and having them write to their legislators is sometimes referred to as 'grass-roots' lobbying. If you make the election under section 501(h), in addition to the total limitation of what you can spend to lobby, you will have a separate limitation on the amount you can spend on 'grass-roots' lobbying."

A lot of advocacy commonly conducted by charities does not rise to the level of lobbying. Save the Chipmunks can attempt to influence the action of government officials aside from legislative decisions, advocate its views through public interest litigation, convene conferences on public policy issues even if those issues are controversial, and express its views on those issues through advertisements, all without necessarily engaging in lobbying as the IRS understands the term.[16]

May not support or oppose candidates for public office. Save the Chipmunks *cannot* do anything that would support or oppose anyone running for office. The IRS considers this prohibition to be absolute.

Having said that, a variety of activities by charities have been found not to constitute prohibited electioneering. For example, where students in a political science course had to participate in political campaigns of their own choosing as part of their course work, or where the student newspaper published student-written editorials on political matters, the IRS ruled that the college was not itself partici-

---

15. The 501(h) election is made by filing Form 5768, Election/Revocation of Election by an Eligible Section 501(c)(3) Organization To Make Expenditures To Influence Legislation. For more information on the expenditure limit or the no substantial amount limit, see IRS Publication 557, Tax-Exempt Status for Your Organization.

16. See IRS Pub 1828 for good discussion of this. Although this publication is aimed at religious organizations, most of the discussion is applicable to exempt organizations in general.

pating in a political campaign. Furthermore, certain nonpartisan voter educational activities are permitted. Where all members of Congress are included in a summary of voting records on legislation on a wide range of topics, and neither the content nor the presentation of the publication implies or expresses an opinion as to the member or the vote, the publication does not constitute prohibited political activity. However, where the publication limits its focus to particular issues of importance to the organization, this would probably cross over the line into prohibited activity.

"What if I decide I want to support someone running for office? Don't I have a constitutional right to do this?"

"Sam, you have a personal right to support or oppose anyone running for political office. But a trade-off for being able to receive charitable contributions that are deductible is that Save the Chipmunks cannot use any of these charitable funds for political activity.

If you want your organization to be able to engage in some political activity, you could establish the organization as a 501(c)(4) social welfare organization. In fact, sometimes 501(c)(3) organizations have sister organizations that are 501(c)(4)s. You need to make sure that the assets of the (c)(3) are not used for (c)(4) purposes, and that the (c)(4) has reasons other than political activity for its existence.

Your chamber of commerce can also engage in some political activity. But, since you cannot get a tax deduction for amounts used for political purposes, the funds given to a (c)(6) like your chamber, for which a business deduction is otherwise available, cannot be used without going through a complex allocation process that limits the total business deduction. As a result, most of these organizations establish a separate PAC, or political action committee."[17]

Establishing Federal Exemption

"How much time do I have to file with the IRS to establish the exempt status of Save the Chipmunks?"

"An organization wanting to be exempt under section 501(c)(3) should file as soon as possible, so you can tell people who might be interested in donating that the organization is exempt. But as long as you file within 27 months from the date of incorporation, the exemption will be retroactive to the date of incorporation."

"What if, for some reason, Save the Chipmunks does not file within 27 months of filing its Articles of Incorporation?"

"If you have a good reason for not filing within the 27-month period, you should provide the IRS with the reason and ask that they waive the 27-month requirement. In fact, the 2004 version of form 1023 has a schedule for the organization to complete if it is filing more than 27 months after incorporation. The IRS will waive the requirement if they think the reason is legitimate, and it is clear that the organization has indeed been organized and operated as an exempt organiza-

---

17. This is a very simple explanation of a very complex topic. If an organization desires to become involved in the political process, it is extremely important to obtain assistance from an attorney who specializes in this area. For more information, see the IRS's Political Organization Home Page: http://www.irs.gov/charities/political/index.html and other sources set forth in Appendix B.

tion during that time. However, if the IRS does not waive the 27-month filing requirement, then the exemption will not begin until the date the IRS receives your filing. Therefore, it would be appropriate to get the application on file as soon as possible."

Donations prior to establishment of exempt status. "Can people donate to Save the Chipmunks before we get a determination letter from the IRS?"

"Yes. People may give to your organization at any time. However, although people may make contributions before you have established your exempt status, you must let them know that your application has not yet been approved; and that until it is, their contributions may not be deductible."

"Should we state in our literature that we have applied for the IRS exemption and are awaiting results?"

"You must make sure you are not mischaracterizing your exempt status. If you have decided to apply for 501(c)(3) status, then you need to let people know that, although you are in the process of applying, or your application is pending with the IRS (if, indeed, you have filed it), it has not yet been granted. You can also tell them (if true) that you have no reason to believe the exempt status will not be granted and, if you have applied within 27 months, that, if granted, the exemption will be retroactive to the date of incorporation. You certainly may make this disclosure in your literature, as long as you are prepared to change it once the exempt determination letter is issued.

Again, once the exempt determination letter is issued, the exemption is retroactive to the date of incorporation as long as you have filed within 27 months of the date of incorporation (and why wait—it won't take any longer to do the work now than it will in 27 months). If you wait longer than 27 months, you may be able to be able to convince the IRS to make it retroactive; otherwise it will be effective as of the date of filing."

Filing for exemption. For a determination of exempt status under most sections other than 501(c)(3), application is made by filing Form 1024, "Application for Recognition of Exemption Under Section 501(a)" with the IRS.

For organizations that want a federal determination of exempt status as a section 501(c)(3) charitable organization, application is made by filing Form 1023, "Application For Recognition of Exemption" with the IRS.

All applications are now required to be filed in Cincinnati, Ohio (mailing address is Covington, Kentucky). From there, they are assigned to an available examiner, either in Ohio, or in another IRS office, for review. Processing time is based both on the workload of the IRS and the difficulty of the particular application. If the situation is straightforward and qualification is obvious, the application may be approved quickly once an examiner has a chance to review the file. If the application has some unusual twist to it, or if the examiner does not understand or is concerned about the exempt character of the proposed activities, even otherwise routine applications may take longer.

Expedited handling. The IRS will consider requests for expedited consideration with appropriate and documented reasons; simply wanting to get to the front of the line is not enough. For example, if a grant is pending and failure to get the grant may have an adverse impact on the organization's operations, or if the purpose is to provide disaster relief to victims of emergencies such as hurricanes or floods, this may be considered a compelling reason for expedited consideration.

To request expeditious handling, include a separate letter, explaining the need. This will be placed immediately before the application itself. Any cover letter should state that "expeditious handling is requested." In addition, all fees must be received before a request will be forwarded for handling.[18] More importantly, the application must be complete; if there is anything missing from the filing, the likelihood of obtaining expeditious handling drops precipitously.

Public Charities v. Private Foundations

"Okay, I think I understand. But I have another question. If I call my organization "Save the Chipmunks Foundation," does that make it a private foundation? And does that change my 501(c)(3) status?"

"In answer to your first question, Sam, the use of the word 'foundation' in an organization's name has no impact on its status. In fact, it has no legal significance. If you think that adding 'foundation' to the name of the corporation is beneficial from a public relations standpoint, or if you just like that name better, you are free to use it.

"But you have pointed to a common misunderstanding about what are called 'private foundations.' All 501(c)(3) organizations are divided into two spheres: private foundations and organizations that are not private foundations (commonly called public charities). When we file to establish your exempt status, we will have to address this issue."

Essentially, one or a few individuals support private foundations, whereas public charities have a broad base of support from the public. But all of these organizations, even those found to be private foundations, continue to be exempt under section 501(c)(3). In fact, many people decide to have their charities classified as private foundations because they have sufficient funds to carry out their purpose, and they do not want to do any significant fundraising.

Because one or a few persons support a private foundation, the contributors will often have substantial control or influence over the use of the money, either directly (for example by being in control of the board) or indirectly (by making certain demands about the use of the donated funds).

As a result of abuses caused by assets being used in a manner that benefited the donors, individuals related to the donors, or friends of the donors, the Code was amended a number of years ago to include specific requirements that private foundations must meet. The special rules are to assure that the funds are used for charitable purposes and not to support the donors' noncharitable special interests.

For example, private foundations must spend a certain amount of their funds each year, they must obtain specific approval from the IRS for any scholarship programs they have, and the reporting and filing requirements are somewhat different than for other (c)(3) entities.

There are certain nonprofits that are automatically found not to be private foundations, such as churches, hospitals, and schools. If an organization falls into this category, it does not need to be concerned about where its funds originate.

---

18. Rev. Proc. 2000-14; 2000-11 IRB 115, Section 9.03(3).

Other nonprofits may be able to show that they are "supporting" organizations of another exempt organization. These nonprofits derive their exempt status from the organization they support. Many "friends of" organizations fall in this category. To be considered a supporting organization, sufficient ties between the supporting organization and the supported organization must be present to assure the IRS that the supported organization will exercise enough supervision over the supporting organization to assure that funds will not be incorrectly used. One way to do this is for the board of directors of the supporting organization to be elected by the supported organization's board.

All other (c)(3)s must either demonstrate that a significant portion of the donations, or a significant portion of the income they receive from exempt organization activities, is derived from the general public.[19]

"I wish I had enough money to fund the organization myself," said Sam. "But I think we will have to raise additional funds to have enough money to accomplish the goals of the organization. You said that we would have to demonstrate this to the IRS when we apply for exemption. Once this is done and the IRS agrees, does this mean I will not need to be concerned about private foundation status in the future?"

IRS Advance Ruling Period

As we noted, all 501(c)(3) organizations are considered to be private foundations unless they fall into specific categories (e.g., school, church, supporting organization), or can actually *show* that they are publicly supported. If you are not one of these organizations, but you have made enough of a showing to convince the IRS that you will probably be a public charity, you will be issued an exempt determination letter with this classification. However, this is not a final determination of your status as a public charity.

Your organization will be given five years to build public support, rather than having to show that the organization has acquired this support from day one. The exempt determination letter will state when this period ends, and a filing is due several months later that will confirm whether or not the organization is publicly supported. During this time, the organization will be treated as not being a private foundation.

At the end of this time, the organization must provide the IRS with the figures they need to determine its level of public support. So Sam needs to continue to be concerned about whether his corporation is or is not a private foundation, and he and his organization need to keep adequate records of where the money comes from so that he will be able to show the level of public support.

This same information will be disclosed on the information form that is filed with the IRS each year (Form 990), so the need to maintain an appropriate level of public support will be ongoing.

If, by the end of the five-year "advance ruling" period, the organization is not able to show that it is publicly supported, it will be reclassified as a private

---

19. This is another complex area. Section 509 of the Internal Revenue Code and regulations outline the tests that must be met if an organization is to be considered a public charity.

foundation. It will continue to remain tax-exempt as an organization under section 501(c)(3), but will have to meet the requirements of a private foundation.

"Okay. What about if we get most of our money from other exempt organizations, rather than individuals? I have been in contact with several other exempt organizations that like what Save the Chipmunks plans to do and may provide some or all of our initial operating budget. Can we receive nonprofit status if we get most of our money from another nonprofit? And will that make us into a private foundation?"

"You can still be exempt if you receive funds from other nonprofits. If the funding nonprofit is publicly supported, the funds, when received by your organization, will still be considered to be public support. However, if the funding nonprofit is a private foundation, then all of the funds from that organization must be treated as being received from one person in determining the level of public support (i.e., if the organization providing the money is a private foundation and most of your money comes from this source, you may also find that your organization has been converted into a private foundation).

"A large gift that could change the balance of whether you are publicly supported may be able to be excluded from your computation, if it is a one time unusual gift.

"It is important to report your sources of support accurately on the forms 990 filed during your advance ruling period, as you might end up having to explain any contradictory allocations. I would suggest that you have us review your 990s before you file them,

"This is an extremely complex area. If there is any question concerning your level of public support, we need to talk BEFORE the end of the advance ruling period, so that we can determine if there are any steps you can take to improve the chances of the organization being found to be publicly supported. It might be a good idea to have us review your records six months or so before the end of the advance ruling period for this purpose."

Obtaining State Exemption

Some states, such as California and Pennsylvania, require all nonprofits to apply for and obtain a tax-exempt determination letter from the state prior to being exempt from taxation and prior to contributions being deductible for state tax purposes (these states conduct an independent review from the IRS). This process requires much of the same information as the Internal Revenue Service determination. Other states accept the IRS determination. Some states, such as Louisiana, require a copy of the IRS determination letter to be filed with the state; others require a separate application with a limited review process. Annual filing requirements also vary by state.

Just because an organization is considered exempt under federal law, it will not necessarily be exempt under state law. When applying for exempt status, the state law should be reviewed to make sure that the organization qualifies for exemption.

If the organization works in more than one state, each state's requirements must be met.

Sometimes a state exemption is granted, contingent upon the organization applying for and receiving exemption from the IRS.

Property Tax Exemptions

The property tax treatment of exempt organizations depends on the use that is made of the property. This aspect of taxation is exclusively a matter of state law. All 50 states have some sort of property tax exemption for property held by organizations exempt under section 501(c)(3).

It should not be assumed that the property of an exempt organization is automatically exempt. A filing may have to be made for each of the exemptions claimed. In some states the filing must be made every year.

If a portion of the property is used for the production of unrelated business taxable income or if it is rented to a business entity or if it is simply left vacant and is not used for the organization's charitable purpose, then the organization may lose the exemption, or may only be entitled to a partial exemption.

Again, property tax exemptions are a matter of state law. If the organization has property in several states, each state law should be reviewed to determine the exempt status of each parcel.

Sales and Use Taxes

As with property tax exemptions, sales tax exemptions are a matter of state law. In some states there is no or only a very limited exemption from sales tax; in others it is very broad.

Business License Taxes

In some states, nonprofits are not regarded as businesses and need not obtain a business license. Other states or municipalities may require the nonprofit to register, but not pay the tax. However, even if a nonprofit is found to be exempt from registration, the municipality may require a business license for non-501(c)(3) activities.

Group Exemption

After his last meeting with Alvin, Sam met with Pastor Ray, the new minister of Oak Street Church. Sam mentioned that, to his knowledge, the church did not have an exempt determination letter from the IRS. Since Sam was working on an exemption application for Save the Chipmunks, he thought maybe he could help the church get one as well. Pastor Ray expressed his concern, and wondered if the church was in jeopardy, particularly since it also operated a private religious school ("Oak Street School"). He asked the church secretary to follow up on this.

The secretary did some digging and discovered that in its 40-year history, the church had never applied for 501(c)(3) status (nor had the school in its 20-year history). A little surprised, she did some calling around, including placing a call to the legal affairs department of the denomination's headquarters. She was told that it wasn't necessary for the church to apply either as a church or school since both were covered under the denomination's group exemption. Pastor Ray and Sam decided it was time to contact Alvin to clarify this matter.

"Can our church and school legally be considered a 501(c)(3) under the umbrella of our denomination?"

"Many churches obtain group exemptions from the IRS, which allow all of the individual churches and other related entities, such as the church school, to be covered. The headquarters church is responsible to regularly provide the IRS with an updated list of organizations that are to be included.

"However, even if there was no group exemption, as I told Sam earlier, churches do not have to obtain an exempt determination letter to be exempt. The only problem with not having such a letter, either an individual letter of exemption or coverage under a group letter, is that if an individual contributor is audited and the contribution is questioned, it is up to the contributor to prove that he or she gave to an exempt organization."

"What are the disadvantages we face as an institution by not having an individual 501(c)(3) status?"

"If the church were to break away from the denomination, it would no longer be covered by the group exemption. As long as it is a part of the denomination, there is really no problem."

"Can the school, as a division of the church, seek separate 501(c)(3) status WITHOUT fully incorporating or splitting off from the parent organization?"

"No. The school is a part of the church. The church, itself, may establish its exemption separate and apart from the denomination, but the school, as a part of the church, cannot. The school would have to be a separate legal entity in order to establish its exempt status separately."

Summary of Fourth Step: Establish Exempt Status

Determine whether the organization will qualify as exempt and if so, under what section of the IRC.	Over 25 different categories. Some of the most common are:	
	Section 501(c)(4)	Social welfare organization; charitable in nature. Most of the same laws apply as with 501(c)(3); however, it can engage in some political activity and can benefit a smaller group of people than the (c)(3). No charitable contribution deduction.
	Section 501(c)(5)	Agricultural, labor organizations.

	Section 501(c)(6)	Chambers of commerce, business leagues. Contributions can generally be deducted as business expenses. The organization cannot benefit a particular business (e.g., Midas Muffler Dealers found to benefit Midas), but may be limited either geographically or professionally. Some political activity permitted, but funds so spent may decrease business expense deduction available.
	Section 501(c)(7)	Social clubs. Must derive most of its income from its members.
	Section 501(c)(3)— Contributions are deductible	Must have one or more exempt purposes.
		Must be organized exclusively for exempt purposes.
		Must be operated exclusively for exempt purposes.
		No net earnings or assets may inure to the benefit of any private person.
		Lobbying—only an insubstantial part of its activities may include attempting to influence legislation.
		No Political activity—may not support or oppose candidates for public office.
Establish Exempt Status	If organization wishes to establish exempt status under section *other than* 501(c)(3)	File Form 1024 with Internal Revenue Service (note: this is optional).
	To establish exempt status under section 501(c)(3)	File Form 1023 with Internal Revenue Service.
		Must be filed within 27 months of incorporation.
		Donations may be made prior to establishing exempt status, but must advise donors that determination of exempt status has not yet been received.
	Group exemption— alternative to separate filing	May be obtained by "parent organization." Allows affiliated organizations to be recognized as exempt without a separate filing by each organization.

Determine source of financial support	Ongoing requirement for 501(c)(3) organizations	If from one or a few sources, may be a private foundation; else it is not a private foundation, often called a public charity.
		At end of Advance Ruling Period, a public charity must show IRS that it continues to qualify for this classification.
Other Tax Issues	Obtain state exemption	Many states recognize IRS exemption; some states require separate filing to establish exempt status.
	Obtain property tax exemption	Controlled by state law. Each state has its own requirements for exemption and its own filing requirements.
	Sales and use taxes	Controlled by state law.
	Business license taxes	Either state or local law. Charitable organizations are often exempt.

PART **II**

Operating Your Nonprofit

After completing all of the organizational steps (incorporating, drafting and adopting bylaws, electing directors and having the initial meeting, establishing the exempt status of the organization with the IRS), Save the Chipmunks is ready to begin operations. Sam has bid Alvin goodbye and is off to seek fame and fortune.

Unfortunately for him (perhaps fortunately for Alvin) Sam has discovered quickly that the legal issues facing his organization have only just begun. Problems with the board, a need to make changes to the organizational documents, questions regarding charitable contributions, issues with both volunteers and employees, reporting requirements for the organization, limitations on how he can raise, spend, and invest money, a notice from the IRS that it intends to audit his corporation, and controversy over his new Internet operations have threatened to derail all of his best efforts. He is discovering that by talking to a competent attorney *before* signing documents might actually be cheaper than trying to save money by doing things himself. Can Sam keep his organization afloat?

Raising and Spending Money

Designated Gifts

"I have been able to raise a lot of money to buy land for conservation purposes, and for scientific research into the breeding habits of chipmunks. There isn't any problem with taking a portion of these funds to cover the operational expenses of the organization, is there?" Sam asks at his next meeting with Alvin.

"Well, Sam," Alvin replies, "it depends upon what representations you made when you raised the money."

43

"Did you tell the contributors that a percentage of the funds would be used for operational purposes? Or did you represent that 100% of these funds would go to the purpose for which they were raised?"

"Alternatively, did you include some sort of language in the solicitation that provided that the directors reserved the right to use the funds for whatever purpose they saw fit?"

"I just copied a check the box envelope that I got from another organization, substituting our purposes for theirs. Hardly anyone designated the funds to go to wherever the need was greatest. They all wanted their money to be used for the specific purposes. But if we can't pay the phone bill, we won't be able to do the research or buy the property."

Sam, you just learned several valuable lessons about fundraising. The first is that if you raise money for a specific purpose, you must use those funds for that purpose. It may be better to raise the funds for general purposes, or to put a qualifying notice on the envelope that allows you to reallocate the funds if necessary to fulfill the purpose. But if someone gives for a specific purpose and you accept the funds with that limitation, you are required to use the funds for that purpose.

"You may be able to go back to the donors and have them authorize a change in purpose; otherwise, depending on state law, you may need a court authorization and/or approval from the Attorney General before you can use the assets for a purpose other than that for which they were contributed."

"The second lesson you have learned is that nonprofits need funds to cover their overhead. No nonprofit has the ability to devote 100% directly to a cause without any portion of it going to overhead; if such a representation is made, it can only be met if the nonprofit has funds from another source to cover overhead."

There is something else Sam may want to do. For restricted assets, Sam might want to have one or more separate accounts (there could be one General Account and one Restricted Fund account, with subdivisions for each specific purpose; or each purpose could have its own restricted fund account). In any event, the restricted account(s) would be limited to funds to be used only for specific purposes.

In addition to providing a level of accountability, this division may also provide some sort of protection against general creditors of the organization as well as inadvertent mistakes by well-meaning employees or volunteers.

Designated Gift to Person

"So I have a related issue. I have a good friend who is terminally ill and I have a group of friends who want to provide money to help out the family. Can Save The Chipmunks do this?"

"Sam, you have two different issues here. The first is that Save the Chipmunks is not formed for the purpose of providing assistance to individuals in need. You must use all of the assets of the organization to fulfill the purpose of the organization. If people make a contribution to your organization contingent upon it being used for another purpose, you cannot accept the contribution."

"I thought you might say that. What about if I set up another exempt organization for the purpose of helping this family?"

"That brings us directly to the second issue, Sam. If your friends want to give money directly to the family, they may, but they will not get a charitable contribution. If they give the money to a charitable organization, they can get a charitable contribution, but they cannot require that the funds go to the family. A donor may designate a specific purpose (e.g., assisting families in need), but cannot designate a specific person.

"Donors can *request* but cannot *require* that funds be used to benefit the family or to pay some of their expenses. It will be up to the charity to determine such issues as 1) whether the family truly needs this type of assistance; and 2) whether this is the best use of the funds (e.g., if they have several other families in similar circumstances, is another one more in need? etc.).

"The charity also cannot simply pass through funds it receives (what if it gets twice as much as the family actually needs?), but should exercise control over the expenditures.

"In any event, you will not be able to form a charitable organization only to benefit this one family, and expect contributions to be deductible."

Restrictions on Contributions: Donor Advised Funds

Sam, in his continuing quest for contributions, has come into Alvin's office with a new possibility: "I have another potential donor who wants to set up what he calls a 'donor advised fund.' He said he could give my organization $100,000 and get a charitable contribution deduction now, but he would tell me later what he wanted to have done with the money. He also wants to have a say in how the money is invested before it is spent. This would really increase our bottom line, so I want to do it. Are there any problems?"

"Well, Sam, before you decide to do this, you need to understand what a donor advised fund is and what it isn't, and when someone may want to use one. Donor advised funds are one of the fastest growing developments in charitable giving, and one of the least understood areas. There is no reference to donor advised funds in the Internal Revenue Code, and there are only a few cases that use the term."

"Essentially a donor advised fund is a contribution to a charity, whereby the charity and the donor agree that, although the assets are given outright to the charity, the charity will consider the donor's wishes when it comes to spending the money."

"Donor advised funds are being used as an alternative to either a private foundation or a supporting organization."

"Remember, we talked about the fact that a charity with one or a few donors (i.e., a private foundation) can be a 501(c)(3) exempt organization? Someone setting up a donor advised fund could use a private foundation for the same purpose—they can give the money now and the private foundation can spend it in the future in the manner the donor directs. But many contributors do not want the responsibilities of running their own private foundation and making sure it complies with all the complex legal and tax requirements."

"A supporting organization may also be used instead of a private foundation. It is considered to be a public charity because of its relationship with the exempt supported organization(s) and thus does not have to follow the complex rules of private foundations. However, the supporting organization is limited, in that it has to list the organization(s) to be supported at the time it is formed, rather than deciding, after the fact, what organizations will benefit. There are also limitations on the ability of a contributor to control the supporting organization."

"A donor advised fund solves some of these problems. Because the money is given to a public charity, there is no separate organization to take care of, and the private foundation requirements do not apply. Further, there is no problem with designating a purpose or organization after the contribution is made."

"The principal IRS issue is whether or not the donor has surrendered enough control to warrant a current contribution deduction, or whether the deduction must wait until there is a distribution from the fund to its final distributee. An organization must actually own and control the funds when the contribution is made for it to be deductible. Once the donation is made, the donor may advise as to the use of those funds, but cannot direct the use. If the organization does not clearly own and control the funds, then a contribution deduction is premature and will not be allowed until the funds are clearly in the possession and control of an exempt organization (e.g., when the donor directs the funds be distributed)."

"One condition that may show the donor has *not* surrendered sufficient control is a provision in the instrument allowing the donor to retain investment control. The donor cannot control how the funds are invested and still get a current charitable contribution. If this is a deal breaker, then the donor may want to set up his or her own charitable organization, either as a private foundation or a supporting organization."

"Although you clearly want to take the donor's desires into account with regard to the actual use of the funds, the organization itself is responsible to see that the funds are used for a charitable purpose. For example, Save the Chipmunks may want to confirm that each recommended recipient is a qualified public charity."

"And, of course, there is still the issue of how giving to the recommended recipient advances the purposes of your organization. It would be best, of course, if the purposes and recipients will somehow be related to your exempt purpose. For example, you might encourage distribution requests to environmentally friendly organizations."

"Another issue is whether a minimum amount must be distributed each year. Some organizations require at least 5% of the assets to be spent annually, since this is what would be required of a private foundation, and they will designate the distributee directly if the donor does not indicate a preference. Or, since you are looking at this as a method of increasing your assets, you must also decide whether or not to include a limit on the maximum amount that will be distributed in a given year."

Some organizations also limit the existence of the donor advised fund—perhaps allowing the original donors to recommend distributions during their lives, and to designate a successor for this purpose, but requiring that all funds remaining upon the death of the successor designee become part of the general fund of the organization.

Contributions of Gifts in Kind

"I have another contributor that wants to give us his used computer equipment and take a deduction for the contribution. Is that legal? What if we don't need the equipment, and decide to sell it after he gives it to us? We could then use the proceeds to cover operating expenses."

"Yes, Sam, it is 'legal.' The question is how much benefit the donor will actually receive. If you use the property, the donor's deduction will be the fair market value of the property. However, if you sell rather than use the property, the deduction of the donor is limited to the lower of the donor's basis (remaining undepreciated cost or other basis in the equipment) and the fair market value (likely to be very low).

"If the donation has a value of $5,000 or more, the donor will have to file form 8283 with the IRS, which the organization must sign (acknowledging the gift, not agreeing with the appraised value). In that case, if the organization sells the equipment within two years, it must file form 8282 with the IRS showing how much it received on the sale of the property. Of course, the result is that if your donor shows a $10,000 contribution deduction and the assets are sold for $500, the IRS will know and your donor will be extremely unhappy to learn he has gotten a free IRS audit for his 'benevolence.'"

"What about having donors give us cars? I keep hearing ads telling me I should give my used car or boat to some charity."

"Sam, this is an area of major concern to the IRS, as people have been donating their used vehicles and taking deductions far in excess of what is actually realized by the charity. As a result, the rules changed on January 1, 2005. Now, if the charity sells the vehicle and the claimed value exceeds $500, the donor is limited to a deduction equal to the gross proceeds actually realized from the sale. The charity has 30 days to let the donor know what this amount is. Only if the charity significantly uses or materially improves the vehicle, may the donor still deduct the vehicle's market value."

"Wow. That is a real change in the law."

"It sure is, Sam."

Borrowing Money

"Okay, you're going to like this one," Sam says, a month later. "I talked with some of my friends, and a number of them are willing to lend Save the Chipmunks money so that we can buy an office building. Save the Chipmunks will use one of the offices, and rent the rest of the space for enough money to pay back the money we borrowed. I figure within five years we should have it paid off, and then we won't have to pay rent anymore, and we will be able to use more money towards helping the chipmunks. So is that a good idea, or what?"

"Okay, take a deep breath, Sam. Let's break this down so we can decide if this is something you really want to do. First, how many lenders are we talking about here?"

"I don't know—anywhere between 10 and 45, depending on how much each person wants to lend, what we buy, and how much money we will need. I told them we should be able to pay them more than they are making at the bank, and they were all interested in investing. David said his mother had a trust fund that is only making 1.5% right now, and that he was sure she would want to participate. Oh, and I almost forgot—I figured that we could use some of the funds to pay the operating expenses until we raise the money for the general fund."

"So you want to borrow money from 10-45 investors, at least one of whom is a widow with a trust fund. You will use this money to buy a building that you will rent to others. You will also use this money for operating expenses. Have I missed anything?"

"No, I think that summarizes it."

"I hate to tell you this, Sam, but if you borrow money with the expectation that you will repay it, you will be issuing securities. Unless there is an exemption available, you may have to register the securities before you can sell them. You may also have to be registered as a sales person, and in some states Save the Chipmunks would have to register as an issuer dealer. The more people from whom you intend to borrow, and the lower their level of sophistication, the more chance that registration will be necessary. Even if registration is not needed, you must provide each investor with all the relevant facts. And if you fail to register, or do not provide enough disclosure, you may be subject to both criminal and civil penalties if the deal goes sour."

"But the deal is not going to go sour," Sam said petulantly.

"If you cannot even raise the money now to cover your operating expenses, how do you expect to raise the funds necessary to cover not only your future operating expenses, but also the past expenses you paid with borrowed money? If you borrow money to purchase a building, then at least the borrowers will have some security that there are assets to make good on their investment. But if you borrow to pay past due funds, what security is there that they will recover their investment?"

"We will have the rent payments from others to cover the payments due on the notes. I penciled it out and it works."

"And what happens when you have a vacancy? Or if you end up paying off your bills and not having enough left over to even purchase the building?"

"And have you included taxes in your figures? If you rent property that is 'debt financed,' a portion of the rent equal to the percentage of the building that is debt financed will be considered income unrelated to your purpose, upon which taxes will be due (Refer to Part II, Raising and Spending Money, Unrelated Business Income).

"Sam, the securities laws are sometimes called 'blue sky' laws. That is because people came up with deals that offered nothing but blue sky—pure optimism at its best. But when it rains—when the deal goes sour, then real people get hurt. The blue sky laws are designed to prevent this. What will you tell your friend, David, if you can't repay his mom?

"If you are going to borrow money, we need to be very specific about what you are borrowing and what will be done with the money. We will also need to design a realistic plan to repay your investors. And most importantly, we need to make sure that you have complied with all applicable securities laws before any money changes hands.[20] Otherwise, in addition to losing David as a friend, you might find yourself facing both criminal and civil penalties."

Sam sighed. "Doesn't anything have an easy answer?"

---

20. See "Chapter 34, Nonprofit Debt Securities and State Regulation," *Nonprofit Governance and Management*, ABA, 2002 for a summary of state securities laws. This article was written specifically with regard to securities issued by religious organizations but provides a good overview of this area.

Purpose and Arrangements with Business Entities

"So what can I do for you today, Sam?"

"You know how you were talking about the problems I might have in borrowing money to buy a building?"

"Yes, Sam, I remember."

"I would like you to meet my brother-in-law, Joe. Joe has a possible arrangement with a business that he thinks might work. But I thought he should come in and meet with you before going forward. I don't want him going to jail because he didn't do everything right."

"Hello, Joe. I think I remember Sam talking about you. Don't you have a non-profit that aids delinquent teenagers?"

"You sure have a good memory, Alvin. I don't even remember talking about Joe."

"So what's the deal, Joe?"

"My nonprofit has developed a rehabilitation plan that is proving to be successful in rehabilitating first-time offenders. A business that reviewed it was impressed, and has suggested a joint venture to make our plan more readily available on a broader scale.

"Under their proposal, a limited liability company, owned 50-50 by Joe's Home for Delinquent Boys and the business, would make rehabilitation services available on a fee-for-service basis. We would provide the program and control the services, while the business would provide financing, develop the centers, handle the administration, and develop a marketing plan to bring in clients.

"After talking to Sam, it sounded like this venture might have some of the same problems as Sam's proposed office building venture. Can we do it? Our nonprofit does not have the equity to do this directly, but I think that the venture would clearly allow us to help more children than we could otherwise."

"Joe, as you probably know, nonprofits must use their assets to advance their purpose. Sometimes the only way to do this is to hire people, or to enter into arrangements with business entities. This is perfectly legitimate *if* the purpose of the nonprofit side is advanced, and *if* the return to the business entity is reasonable. Both of these are big 'ifs.'

"Your nonprofit needs to maintain sufficient control to assure that your non-profit purpose is advanced. If the activity turns out to be your nonprofit's primary activity, to assure that your exempt status is not jeopardized, your nonprofit should maintain control over the entire project. If the activity is an ancillary activity, then your nonprofit should maintain control over the aspects of the activity that would assure that the nonprofit purpose is carried out.

"Because your organization must use its assets to advance its nonprofit purpose, there must be some assurance that the business entity will not unreasonably benefit from the arrangement, taking into consideration the services and funding provided by the business. If the purpose (or the net effect) is to provide an unreasonable benefit to the business, then this is not only improper, it may result in the loss of your exempt status, as well as the imposition of penalties on both the recipient of the unreasonable benefit (i.e., the business), and those that authorized the same (i.e., you and your directors)." (Refer to Part II, Enforcement of Laws, Intermediate Sanctions.)

"Having said all of this, the specific terms of the joint venture between Joe's Home for Delinquent Boys and the business will determine whether either of these principles are violated. It is not clear, for example, whether the proposed joint venture will turn out to be the principal activity of the nonprofit. If it is an ancillary venture, then the proposed level of control may be sufficient, as the nonprofit maintains control over the actual program and service.

"We also need more information to decide if the return to the business is reasonable. It is likely that this will have to be decided on a facts and circumstances basis. Once we know all of the specifics about the proposal, we will be able to evaluate it. Of course, there is no guarantee that the business will want to proceed with the venture if it cannot obtain the terms that it wants. But if it is not drafted correctly, then you will be endangering your entire program.

"Another issue is whether or not you will be personally benefiting from this."

"It's interesting that you mention that. I did not think that I would get anything beyond my regular salary, but they suggested that perhaps the LLC could hire me for my expertise. I'm not sure what they were thinking."

"You need to make sure that your ENTIRE compensation, whether from your nonprofit or from the LLC, is reasonable in light of your duties and responsibilities, and that you are not personally receiving a benefit that would otherwise go to the nonprofit.

"The bottom line is, although this joint venture may be extremely beneficial to the nonprofit, careful attention must be given to the negotiation of the terms and drafting the actual agreement, so as not to put your exempt status at risk. You will need an attorney to draft the necessary documents, and to make sure that all of these issues are resolved in a manner that will not endanger your tax exempt status."[21]

"Thanks, Alvin. That helps. I will let you know what develops."

Deferred Giving

Since its inception, Sam has concentrated on getting cash contributed to Save the Chipmunks. Alvin has encouraged him in this. Cash can be spent if needed, or saved for future use if not needed immediately. But Sam has recently had a number of people ask about giving money in the future. In fact, several people have let him know that they plan to list Save the Chipmunks as a recipient under their wills. Others have said that they are not in a position to give the money outright, but wondered if there was another way to give. Sam has asked Alvin for some basic information about what types of giving he might suggest to them.

It is important to note that all of the following methods of giving are irrevocable. Once the assets are given and a charitable contribution deduction is taken, the document cannot be changed (other than a change to the charity receiving the benefit or certain changes required to comply with law). The charitable dedication cannot be rescinded. Therefore, unless the individual has money to spare, none of these instruments should be used.

---

21. See *Joint Ventures Involving Tax-Exempt Organizations*, 2nd Edition, 2000 by Michael I. Sanders, John Wiley & Sons, Inc.

Generally, unless there is a specific provision in the Internal Revenue Code that allows an individual to give only a partial interest in an asset (e.g., a 50% interest in a painting), it is necessary that an entire interest be given before a charitable deduction can be taken. The instruments described below are ways to give a partial interest in property that are specifically allowed under the Internal Revenue Code.

Charitable Remainder Trusts

If a person needs to be able to use the income from an asset, but wants to give the remainder to charity and receive a charitable contribution deduction now, he or she can do so using a charitable remainder trust.

Charitable Remainder Unitrust

With a charitable remainder unitrust, the donor(s) contribute assets to the trust, and designate, in the trust instrument, what percentage of assets they wish to receive back each year, and whether the payments will be for a period of years (up to 20 years), or for the rest of their life or lives. The annual percentage paid back must be at least 5%. At the end, the remainder goes to the designated charity(s).

Charitable Remainder Annuity Trust

A charitable remainder annuity trust is the same as the unitrust, except that the amount designated to be received by the donor(s) is a fixed amount, just like a regular annuity, rather than a percentage.

Charitable Lead Trusts

A charitable lead trust is just the opposite of a charitable remainder trust. The charity receives the current income, and the donor or his or her beneficiary receives the remainder at the termination of the trust. For example, if the person does not need the funds now, but wants to leave the remainder to his or her children or grandchildren, a charitable lead trust may be used. A percentage of the assets in the trust is paid to the charity designated by the individual during the term of the trust. The individual gets a charitable contribution for the estimated value of the gift. At the end of the term of the trust, the remainder goes to the individual beneficiaries designated. In addition to getting a charitable contribution, the value of the gift to the beneficiaries is the estimated value of the remainder interest at the time of the transfer of the assets to the trust. Since the remainder interest will not be received by the beneficiaries immediately, its present value is likely to be significantly smaller than the amount actually paid to the beneficiaries at the end of the trust. This was a greater benefit before changes in the federal estate tax law increased the amount excluded from federal estate tax. However, since the reduction in/elimination of the estate tax is not permanent (currently the changes expire in 2010), such a trust may still have benefits, in addition to the current charitable deduction.

Charitable Gift Annuities

A charitable gift annuity is similar in concept to a charitable remainder trust (the individual receives an annuity; the charity receives whatever is left when the annuity terminates). The difference is that the charitable remainder trust is a stand-alone entity, the assets of which must be separately invested and accounted for, whereas the assets of each charitable gift annuity is commingled with the other annuities offered by the same charity. Some states require registration of the charitable gift annuity program before it may be offered.[22]

Remainder Interests in Residence

In each of the above scenarios, the assets funding the trust/annuity must be actually surrendered to the charity for the charitable contribution to be available. The gift of a remainder interest in your residence is the exception to the rule that an entire interest in property must be given before a charitable contribution deduction may be taken. The donor may keep a life interest in the property and continue to live there, while receiving a current deduction for the remainder interest. A problem arises if the donor wants to sell or refinance the house. Because the donor is no longer the sole owner, the property cannot be refinanced, or sold and a new residence purchased, without the consent of the charity, and/or the charity receiving its proportionate interest in the property being sold.

Charitable Contributions to Non-501(c)(3) Exempt Organizations

Recently, the chamber of commerce to which Sam belongs has talked about conducting certain fund-raising campaigns. Sam remembered that Alvin told him that even though the chamber of commerce had an exempt determination letter, this does not entitle individuals to deduct their contributions as charitable contributions, although a business expense deduction may be available. This is because the exempt determination letter received by the chamber clearly reflects that it is exempt under section 501(c)(6) as a business league, chamber of commerce, or similar organization, rather than under section 501(c)(3).

Only contributions to Section 501(c)(3) organizations can be deducted as charitable contributions. The chamber has gotten around this limitation by working directly with certain charitable organizations that it chooses to support and having the contributions made directly to the charity. It has considered whether it should form a "sister" 501(c)(3) instead. Sam has referred them over to Alvin for advice as to whether this can and should be done.

Although the chamber may continue to raise funds for specifically designated nonprofits exempt under 501(c)(3), it is absolutely appropriate, if a (c)(6) is doing a significant amount of charitable type of work, to have a related (c)(3) that can receive donations. This will make the ongoing operations easier, since they will not

---

22. See http://www.pgresources.com/ for more information about this area of law, including registration requirements.

have to establish agreements with the individual charities before engaging in the fund-raising activity. However, the "sister" nonprofit must actually be organized and operated for charitable purposes and must establish its exempt status under 501(c)(3) for the contributions to be deductible.

Another caveat is that, although a non-(c)(3) such as the chamber may give assets to its sister (c)(3), the (c)(3) must make sure that none of its assets are used to benefit the chamber.

Should the Same Entity Be Used for Various Operations?

After a little prodding from Sam, Pastor Ray just called Alvin again.

"Our Board of Elders has approved starting a day care center as an outreach ministry and for the training of children. This fits within the purposes of the church, but the Board is concerned about liability issues, and it wants to limit the financial exposure of the church for this new activity. Would a separate entity for this activity be prudent?"

"There are many reasons to keep either a school or a day care center as a part of the church. If the school or center is located on the church premises, the church will be involved in most lawsuits anyway.

"By keeping the school or center as a part of the church, the church has more control over the operations. It can make sure the school continues to operate as an outreach ministry of the church.

"Further, if the school or center is a part of the church, then it will be covered by the Church Audit Procedures Act[23] whereas if it is separately incorporated, it will not. In addition, if the school or center is a part of the church, in most states, the church/school/center is not subject to unemployment insurance, whereas if the school or center is separately incorporated, the state may press for coverage.

"Unless there are other facts, such as with a school that has outgrown the church facility and wants to purchase its own facility in another location, and a church board that does not want to incur the expense of a separate facility, I would generally suggest the church not spin off the school or day care center. The church should make sure it has adequate insurance coverage, and oversees important aspects of the school where liability might be incurred (such as criminal background checks of the staff)."

"I guess that's probably the deciding factor in our case. The board really made it clear that, although they like the idea of the center, the church should not have ongoing responsibility for it."

"In that case, the child care center would probably be better formed as a separate corporation."

"But if we spin it off into its own corporation, can our church provide the initial financing?"

"Clearly the Oak Street Church, as a 501(c)(3), can give grants to other 501(c)(3) organizations. However, these grants must advance the purposes of the church. As

---

23. See IRC Section 7611. The IRS may not audit a church without complying with specific safeguards. For purpose of this section, a church is any entity claiming to be a church, except that a separately incorporated religious school is specifically excluded.

we have already agreed, a child care center may be an appropriate activity for the church. If the church could do it directly, it certainly can provide support to another organization engaging in the same activity. Many private foundations do not do any charitable work directly, but simply give money away on a regular basis to other (c)(3)s.

"As long as the child care center establishes its exemption under section 501(c)(3), the church can give money to the center and will not need to actively supervise how the money is spent.

"A (c)(3), in some instances, might be permitted to give money to an individual or organization that is not a (c)(3) if, by doing so, its purposes are clearly advanced. For example, many charities give financial assistance and food to needy people. And an organization that has not established its exempt status may still engage in an activity that might be charitable in nature (such as conducting research that it will make available to the general public). However, if the (c)(3) is going to provide funding for such an activity, the (c)(3) must verify that the charitable purpose is served, and that the funds are not used for the private benefit of the individual or non(c)(3) organization. Therefore, if the childcare center has not established its exempt status, then the church must be diligent to exercise what is termed 'expenditure responsibility' over the grant.

"The church cannot give money to another organization, either a (c)(3) or another type of entity, to be used for a purpose that the church could not do itself. For example, (c)(3)s cannot engage in political activity. Therefore, it cannot provide support (including a meeting room or an office) to another organization that engages in political activity."

Support to a Non-U.S. Organization

"I think I understand," Pastor Ray replied. "So at this point, it would be fine to provide financing to form the day care center.

"What about the orphanage we support in Mexico? Our church has been supporting a missionary down there for quite some time. A couple of years ago, he introduced us to the orphanage. We have started to send some of our people down to work at the orphanage and have 'adopted' it, so that at the present time, much of their ongoing operational support is coming from our church. But now they need a new building that will cost more than our church can fund. The board has asked whether we should set up another corporation to solicit contributions for the orphanage from others as well."

"Well, that depends on a couple of things," Alvin replies. "I assume you have made an affirmative determination that your support of the orphanage is consistent with and advances your mission—as part of your religious requirement to take care of widows and orphans. If you have not done so, your board should do so immediately. If this is not the case, I would question whether even the current level of support is appropriate.

"Even if the increased level of support would be permissible as part of your purposes, a separate organization might be beneficial, since it could concentrate on raising funds for the orphanage. Further, some people might be more willing to give to a separate organization than they might be to give to your church.

"Whether the funds are raised by a separate 'friends of' organization or are run though your church, the U.S. entity must exercise 'expenditure control' over any of the funds used outside of the United States. This is true even if the orphanage would qualify as a charity if it were in the United States. In other words, your church or the separate U.S. entity must make sure that the assets are actually being spent for the charitable purpose for which they were raised, just as if you were giving to an individual or a non-501(c)(3) entity. You cannot just give the funds to the orphanage to use as it sees fit.[24]

"Another option is to see if there is an existing U.S. charitable organization, other than your church, that would be willing to channel funds from other sources, thus doing away with the need for a separate organization and avoiding the costs of operating another entity."

Business Entity Raising Funds for Nonprofit Purpose

There is a public relations firm in Sam's town that has been holding a local event to help needy chipmunks. Because the firm has sometimes helped Save the Chipmunks, Sam has been intimately involved in some of these events. The president, Mike Giver, has decided to commit his company to expanding the event nationally. Sam told him that he really should consider establishing a 501(c)(3) organization for this purpose, but Mike has been reluctant to do that, as he really does not like the idea of having another entity to administrate. The question Sam posed to Alvin in his last phone call was, "Since Mike's company is not a charity, can it solicit funds (cash or property) on behalf of the event if a national charity is not involved?"

"Mike can always *ask* for money (as long as he has complied with any solicitation requirements), but he must make sure he lets the potential donor know that the donor may not be entitled to a charitable contribution deduction."

"Well, but how can Mike make sure that donors are able to receive a tax deduction?"

Mike has several choices. The first is to find a charity in each area with which Mike can work to be the recipient of proceeds from the events in that area. All contributions can be made directly to the charity, or the charity can appoint Mike as its agent to solicit and collect the contributions on its behalf. Of course, if Mike is soliciting in the charity's name, the charity needs to exercise "expenditure responsibility" to make sure that the funds are correctly used. In addition, in either of these situations, Mike may have to register in some or all of the states in which he is soliciting contributions. (Refer to Charitable Solicitation Registration below.)

Another option is to find one charity with which to work for all events. It does not have to be operating nationally, but it must be exempt as a 501(c)(3) organization and have a purpose similar to the purpose for which Mike wishes to raise the funds.

Organizations receiving less than $5,000 per year are not required to separately establish their exempt status with the IRS. Therefore, if the total gross receipts are

---

24. What constitutes adequate control of the donated funds is discussed in Rev. Rul. 66-79, 1966-1 C.B. 48. The organization must demonstrate that it has full control of the donated funds and discretion as to their use so as to insure that the funds will be used to carry out the domestic charity's function and purposes. See also Rev. Rul. 75-65, 1975-1 C.B. 79 and GCM 35319 (Apr. 27, 1973).

not more than $5,000 in a year, and Mike clearly separates these receipts from his company's assets (perhaps by forming a trust or an unincorporated association so that it is clearly organized and operated for exempt purposes), and makes sure the assets are used only for charitable purposes, then he might be able to get by without a separate nonprofit entity that has established its exempt status and still have the contributions be deductible. But the problem is that it is then the contributor's burden to prove that he or she gave to an exempt organization. In addition, the possible need to register to solicit funds would still be present.

Charitable Solicitation Registration

"Okay, you have mentioned, several times, charitable solicitation registration. What in the world are you talking about?"

"Many states require that, if you are located in the state or plan to solicit funds from residents of that state, you must register before soliciting funds. Although there may be some exceptions, if you are going to be soliciting funds from the public, you really need to make sure that you have complied not only with the laws of the state in which you are located but of EACH state in which you are soliciting funds."

"Let's see. We file with the Secretary of State. We file with the IRS. In some states we file with the Attorney General. And in addition, we need to file to raise money? Why?"

"The reason is to make sure that the nonprofit is not conducting some sort of scam. Some well-publicized fraudulent activities have been done in the name of nonprofits, which has resulted in this additional level of regulation. The nonprofits that do everything right bear a burden as a result of those who did it wrong."

"Is there some easy way to do this?"

"There is no way you can file one form in one place to take care of all registrations in numerous states. However, many states are recognizing the large burden this can place on a nonprofit. There is now a uniform form that can be used in many states called the 'Unified Registration Statement.' It is available at http://www.multistatefiling.org. This site also lists the states that currently allow the form to be used (including some that require additional information).

"But you need to note that there may be other registrations as well, not included on this site. Hundreds of counties or cities have their own solicitation registration requirements. For example, in California over 200 cities and counties have separate solicitation ordinances.

"Sometimes states also require registration for professional solicitors or fundraisers. This means that if you hire someone to do fund-raising for you, you must determine if that person needs to be registered, and if so, whether or not that person is registered."

Internet Operations

"What if I just include the solicitation on my web page? That does not require registration, does it? I've heard that the Internet is pretty much unregulated; it seems like this would be similar."

"It depends upon what, exactly, you are doing. It is true that if you receive an entirely unsolicited contribution from someone in another state, you could argue that that state has no authority over you. However, as soon as you respond to that contribution by receipting it (which you need to do) or adding that person to your mailing list, you may be found to have slipped over the line into what the state would regard as soliciting.[25]

"Actually, the law concerning nonprofits and the Internet is still evolving. All of the law that otherwise applies is equally applicable to any activities conducted over the Internet. The problem, however is knowing exactly how to apply the law. One problem is that by the time it is clear how a law applies, the actual operations on the Internet have usually morphed into something else."

"What if someone else raises funds for us on their own website? We were approached by Goodpeople.org, who said that they were a nonprofit organization and had a service where we could register with them and have them raise money for us. Would that keep us from having to register?"

"There are several issues here. First of all, Goodpeople.org itself will have to register to solicit charitable contributions where required. It may also have to register as a charitable fund-raiser. Secondly, unless Goodpeople is exempt under 501(c)(3), the only way contributors are entitled to a charitable contribution is if Goodpeople is your agent (preferably with a written agreement), and you receipt the charitable contributions, which would again bring you right back into the same problem. If they are exempt and receipt the contributions directly, so that you do not do anything to communicate with the contributor, then you would not have to register. However, if that happens, you will not have the benefit of having the names and contact information of each contributor, which could be extremely valuable information. Finally, what control do you have over what Goodpeople says about your organization?"

"So we need to know more before we decide to do anything with them."

"Exactly."

Accumulating and Managing Funds

Having finished for the day with Sam, Alvin found that Joe was next on his agenda.

"Alvin, I've got a question," Joe said, getting right to the point. "Joe's Home for Delinquent Boys Auxiliary (a separate exempt organization that has been formed as a "supporting organization" for Joe's Home for Delinquent Boys) has a memorial fund with no designated purpose other than the organization's general purpose "to render support and service to the Home." This fund now has about $1,000,000 accumulated in it at a rather low interest rate (under 5%). I am concerned about how the Auxiliary board is operating, including its current use (or 'non-use') of the funds. Can you provide me with some direction?"

"It sounds like you have a good problem, Joe. You have money that has accumulated, rather than having to live hand-to-mouth like most nonprofits."

---

25. The National Association of State Charity Officials (NASCO) has worked to develop principles to aid both the nonprofits and the regulators (see the "Charleston Principles" at www.nasconet.org.

"Well, yes, but shouldn't the money be used to further the purposes of the organization rather than just left to accumulate? After all, we have been looking at developing some expansion projects, and having use of those funds now could be beneficial."

"Actually, that sounds like a really *good* reason not to spend all of the money now. If the auxiliary is able to continue to raise and accumulate funds, it may be able to actually fund the expansion projects, rather than simply using the funds it raises to develop the plans for the expansion project.

"In addition, putting money in a reserve fund for those times when the organization is less successful at fund-raising may be critical to the success of the organization, rather than spending all of the money now. If I remember correctly, the last time there was a downturn in the market, your ability to raise private donations was severely curtailed, and you had to cut some of your programs. If your organization, or the auxiliary, can build up a reserve, this will allow you to continue your programs, even during the lean years."

"That's true," Joe replied. "I remember that when that happened, there was even more need for our services than normal, and we couldn't help all the children because we didn't have the money."

"You are not wrong to make sure the money is used. In fact, I would recommend that you work with your Auxiliary to establish guidelines as to how much should be accumulated, and for what purpose. Clearly, if the funds are sufficient to cover foreseeable needs, such as your new building project or to provide needed reserves, then the additional funds should be directed for use in a way that accomplishes the purpose for which the funds were given."

"I have another question. Doesn't the board have an 'obligation' to get the highest rate of return on the invested funds? Right now, most of the funds are invested in bank savings accounts. I don't think the interest is even sufficient to keep up with our current rate of inflation."

"Well, the board also has an obligation to invest the funds wisely. It is better to get a consistent return on a secure investment, than to get a high rate of return and potentially lose the investment. For example, the 'New Era'[26] case involved nonprofits that were interested in a good rate of return, but forgot to check out the security of the investment. The interest rate was good, but it turned out to be a ponzi scheme, where money from initial investors was spent by the promoter, money from subsequent investors was used to pay the interest and principal for the earlier investors, and nothing was left to pay the subsequent investors. Many nonprofits lost a significant portion of their investments.

"Depending upon the proposed use of the funds, sometimes it is better to have a lower rate of interest and have the money available immediately rather than to tie the funds up for a longer period of time, even if the interest rate is higher."

Uniform Management of Institutional Funds Act

The Uniform Management of Institutional Funds Act (UMIFA) was drafted by the National Conference of Commissioners on Uniform State Laws to provide

---

26. See *In re Foundation for New Era Philanthropy*, No. 95-13729BIF (Bankr. E.D. Pa. 1995).

a standard of conduct in the management and investing of institutional funds. Prior to this, the law concerning the management of institutional funds, particularly endowment funds, was uncertain. This law provides standards for the investment and expenditure of funds other than assets held for program-related purposes. The concept is that prudence should be exercised both in the investment and the spending of the endowment funds, with an eye towards maintaining the fund in perpetuity. This act has been adopted in 46 states. It is currently in the process of revision.

Is Your Contribution Deductible? You Can't Deduct the Fur Coat

Near the beginning of each year, we all have to face the fact that it is time again to prepare our income tax returns. Joe, Sam's brother-in-law, having made significant contributions to Save the Chipmunks, to his own nonprofit, and to other charitable organizations, is now looking for every possible deduction that may be available. He has come to Alvin to help determine which of his contributions may result in a tax write-off.

Outright donations of money, such as Joe's cash contributions to Save the Chipmunks, continue to be legitimate income tax deductions. These may be listed in their entirety on Schedule A of his tax return.

But what about the suggested donation of $10 that Joe made when he attended the Christmas concert put on by the Oak Street School? Or the $100-a-plate dinner he paid for and planned to attend, but missed because Aunt Matilda flew into town? Or a book written by the CEO of the organization that was given to him when he sent in $50? Or the $20 he contributed to his favorite TV program, in exchange for an autographed photograph of the TV host? What about the $1,000 he paid for the fur coat at the hospital charity auction? Or the $4,000 he had to contribute to the Oak Street School to cover the cost of his child's tuition?

All of these "contributions" have something in common: The donor received a benefit in exchange for the contribution. As a result, the contribution may not be fully, or even partially deductible. **Unless the value of what was received is nominal, then that value must be deducted from the amount contributed to arrive at the allowable deduction.** Let us look at the examples:

"Suggested Donation" to Attend Concert

If $10 must be paid to attend the concert, then it is not a $10 donation. If the actual value of the concert can be shown to be less than $10, the value of the concert must be subtracted from the $10 to determine the appropriate deduction. If the actual value cannot be shown to be less than $10, no donation will be available. For future concerts, Oak Street School should be encouraged to state the value of the concert and the amount of the available deduction. Further, any required payment should not be referred to as a "donation." This is misleading and may be considered by the IRS to be encouraging tax fraud.

Of course, if the concert is truly free and no contribution need be made to attend, then any contribution should be able to be deducted in its entirety. However, unless it can be clearly shown that people understood that the "suggested donation" was strictly voluntary, and that at least some people attended without making such payment, the deduction will likely be denied. It would have been more appropriate to simply encourage attendees to donate (for example, by passing collection plates), so that the amount given would clearly be a deductible gift.

Dinner Missed because Aunt Matilda Flew into Town

If Joe gave the ticket back to the charity before the dinner, he can deduct the entire amount contributed, as no benefits were received. However, if he continued to hold onto the ticket in the event of Aunt Matilda's trip being cancelled, then he must deduct the value of being able to attend the dinner, just as if he had actually attended. As with the concert, the charity should have informed him of the value of the dinner (e.g., $25), so that he would know how much was deductible as a charitable contribution (e.g., $75).

Autographed Photograph of TV Host

If the TV program was conducting a fund-raising campaign and informed Joe of how much of his contribution was deductible, *and* the fair market value of the photograph is nominal, the entire value of his contribution can be deducted. However, if the value of the photograph is substantial, its value must be subtracted from the contribution to determine the amount able to be deducted.[27]

Book by CEO

As with the photograph, if the fair market value of the book is insubstantial ($8.20 or less as of 2004), the entire amount can be deducted. If it is more than insubstantial, the deduction must be reduced by the value of the item received. IRS limitations on how much can be given to a donor without the deductibility of their gift being affected are adjusted each year for inflation. For 2004, the donor may receive something with a fair market value equal to no more than 2% of the contribution OR $82, whichever was less. Alternatively, if the book is a token item and bears the organization's name or logo, then the guidelines still allow the entire amount donated to be deductible. Therefore, if the fair market value of the book is insubstantial, or if the photograph or book is worth a small amount but has the organization's name or logo imprinted on it, his entire donation can be deducted.

Fur Coat from Hospital Charity Auction

If the value of the coat was $600, was clearly marked as such, and Joe paid $1,000, then his available deduction is $400. If the value of the coat was not substantiated,

---

27. See Rev. Rul. 67-246, IRS Publication 1391.

it may be difficult to obtain any deduction. Clearly, if the value is $1000 or more, then no deduction is available.

Mandatory Contribution to School for Child's Tuition

Tuition is never deductible as a charitable contribution. Never. Not ever. Not even if it is called by another name. If the private school is partially or entirely supported by another nonprofit (such as a church), and there is *no* relationship between the amount contributed to the church by the parents and the number of children attending the school, then contributions to the church may be deductible. However, if a "contribution" to the church is based on how many children attend the school, or it can be shown that parents with children attending the school who were not required to pay "tuition" contributed more to the church than those without children attending the school, the conclusion is that this was simply a disguised method of paying tuition, and the deduction is likely to be denied in whole or in part.

Of course, if Joe contributed to a scholarship fund for the benefit of deserving children, and the children benefiting are not related to him or otherwise chosen by him, then the deduction will likely be allowed. However, if his children (or grandchildren), or the child of a close friend benefit, then no deduction is available.

The bottom line is that contributions required in exchange for a benefit are not deductible.

Unrelated Business Income

"So tell me more about unrelated business income tax. I don't want to pay any taxes that I don't have to," Sam asks Alvin the next time they meet.

"Exempt organizations generally do not have to pay taxes on income that they receive, whether the income is made up of contributions or is actually earned by the organization. In some situations, exempt organizations began to operate what were actual businesses that competed with businesses operated by for-profit entities. Of course, in some instances, the 'business' was part of the exempt purposes of the organization, such as the school operated by an educational organization.

"However, in other situations, the 'business' had no exempt purpose and was instituted only to raise money for the organization. Obviously, this disturbed business owners with similar 'for-profit' businesses, since they had to pay taxes on their income earned and thus had a higher overhead, making it difficult for them to compete.

"Congress tried to balance all of these concerns when it developed the concept of an unrelated business income tax (UBIT). Before a tax would be instituted, the business would have to be unrelated to the nonprofit purpose of the organization, *and* the business must be regularly carried on.

"Although this sounds like a relatively simple rule, it becomes difficult to apply in practice.

"Further, there are many exceptions to the rule. For example, a thrift store selling donated items would be exempt from UBIT, even if the business was regularly carried on. A business staffed entirely by volunteers would also be exempt.

"Another common exception is the convenience exception. For example, the college bookstore is found to be operated for the convenience of the students, and therefore any income earned is not subject to unrelated business income tax."

"Does this mean that if the PTA of Oak Street School has a store that sells school supplies and uniforms, there is no unrelated business income? How about if it only operates during the first week of every quarter? Would that mean it is not regularly carried on?"

"Oh, where to start. Sam, this question is a good example of how this area becomes complex very quickly. To begin with, is the PTA a separate nonprofit, or is it operating as part of the Oak Street School?"

"I think it is a part of the school. Why? Does it make a difference?"

"If it is a part of the school, then providing school supplies and uniforms might be very much related to the purpose. If the PTA is a separate entity, then we need to inquire into its purpose to see how it is related.

"Even when the store is operated as part of the school, you will need to look at each of the items being sold to make sure that they are related. If, for example, the store sells items such as key chains and other trinkets, these may not be related, as would the notepaper, pencils, and books.

"But we don't stop our analysis here. Even if some of the supplies are not clearly related to the purpose, there may be another exemption. You mentioned that the store is actually operated by the PTA. Do the parents volunteer their time to run the store, or are they paid?"

"The parents are all volunteers. We also involve the students themselves in doing basic work such as taking inventory, stocking shelves, and balancing the cash register."

"If no one is paid, then you can rely upon the volunteer exception, even if some of the items sold are not clearly related. But you mentioned having the students involved. In this case, it appears that the store is also being used to teach students on a practical level. This would again show that the store and its operations are clearly related to the purpose of the school, even if you had people being paid to operate it.

"We don't have to stop there with the analysis. I mentioned the convenience exception as well. Even if the operations of the store were not clearly related to the purpose of the school, and even if the volunteer exception was not available, if the items being sold are offered for the convenience of the students, this would be another exception to keep the income from being classified as unrelated business taxable income."

"Well, that actually is why we started the store in the first place. The school has a dress code, and we found that parents and students were having difficulty in finding the requisite uniforms. And with growing children, this is an ongoing problem. By having a store on campus, students would not have an excuse to attend in non-conforming outfits, saying that they could not find what they needed."

"Given all of that, we probably do not have to address the question of whether, by limiting the store's operation to the first week of every quarter, the operations would be found to not be regularly carried on. This is just as well, since I am not sure how the IRS would rule. Once a year is clearly not 'regularly carried on;' every day clearly is. There is no bright line in-between to determine the dividing line.

"The bottom line is that if you are doing something that might be considered to be a business, you really need to consult with an expert to see whether and how you can keep it from being categorized as being unrelated business income.

"Even if there is a tax, it is a tax on the profits. The after-tax profits realized by the school are still often better than no profits at all."

Taxability of Investment Income

"What about the interest earned on the funds we have invested? Is that taxable as unrelated business income?"

"It depends on the investment, Sam."

"Passive investments, such as dividends, interest, royalties, and most rents from real property, are normally not taxed unless the income is debt-financed (i.e., you borrowed to make the investment). If you borrowed to make the investment, then the tax would be on that portion that is debt-financed. If you paid $100,000 for real property and owe $50,000 on it, then one-half of your profits would be taxable.

"An active investment, such as income from a partnership (even one that is publicly traded), is probably taxable because the investment is considered to be engaging in business."

Subsequent Bankruptcy of Donor

"Okay, I have a new problem," Sam informed Alvin over the phone. "I had a donor who gave Save the Chipmunks about $20,000 over the past two years. The only problem is that he recently went bankrupt, and the bankruptcy trustee is asking for all of his contributions back. We don't have an extra $20,000 to give him. Does he really have any rights to any of these funds? And if so, where does he expect us to come up with the money?"

"Well, Sam, you might be okay, but we need more information. There have been a number of instances where, after a person declares bankruptcy, the trustee has attempted to, and in many instances, has been successful in requiring contributions to various charities to be put back into the bankruptcy estate, if the contribution was made within one year of the bankruptcy filing.

"In order to provide some protection to the innocent charity, the law was changed to shield some charitable contributions from the reach of the bankruptcy trustee.[28]

"The revised law also allows people in bankruptcy to continue to make charitable gifts, as long as the gifts do not exceed 15% of their income.

"The protected contributions are gifts of cash and financial instruments (e.g., stocks, bonds, options, and derivatives) to certain "religious and charitable" organizations.[29] Save the Chipmunks is a charitable organization, so the first question is, "What was the form of the contributions?"

---

28. In June of 1998, the "CHARITY DONATION PROTECTION ACT." S. 1244, was adopted by the United States Congress.

29. The organizations to which this law applies are 501(c)(3) organizations, contributions to which are deductible under Section 170(c)(1) or (c)(2) of the Internal Revenue Code.

"Well, most of the funds were cash contributions, but he did give us a trust deed for $5,000."

"Contributions of other types of personal property and real property continue to be open to challenge. Therefore, the trustee may have a claim against the $5,000. I am afraid I don't know enough about bankruptcy law to tell you if there are any other defenses you can raise.

"There is another question as well. Did the person give the contributions personally, or did he use a corporation or other entity to funnel the money to Save the Chipmunks? Contributions must be made directly by the individual, and not through a corporation to be protected under this law."

"I don't know that answer to that question. I guess I better check."

"While you are checking this, you might also find out how much the donor gave to charitable organizations before going bankrupt. If, before the bankruptcy, the donor regularly gave more than 15% every year, then the 15% limit on permissible contributions made before the bankruptcy may be increased to correspond with the person's regular giving pattern.

"For example, if the person had given 20% of his income to charity for each of the past 10 years, the 20% he gave in the year of the bankruptcy may be allowed to stand. However if he had only given 10% in past years, and increased it to 20% in the year of the bankruptcy, 5% of those funds will be open to attachment by the trustee.

"The 15% limit on contributions by the individual currently in bankruptcy will not be increased. Even the person who regularly gave 20% before going bankrupt, will not be able to give away more than 15% of his or her income to charity while that person is in bankruptcy."

Reporting Requirements

Form 990

"Sam, it is good to see you! How is your nonprofit going?"

"I'm fine, but I'm not so sure about my corporation. I never was very good at numbers, and now I have been told I need to fill out, not only my own tax returns, but one for Save the Chipmunks as well. I don't even know what form to use. And I thought that because we didn't have any unrelated business income, Save the Chipmunks did not have to pay taxes. What am I missing?"

"Actually, Sam, the basic form you need to fill out for Save the Chipmunks is an 'informational' form, rather than a tax return. It is Form 990, and is available on line at the IRS website.

"As we discussed before, nonprofits may be required to pay taxes—if they run a business that is regularly carried on and which is unrelated to the purpose of the nonprofit. Then the organization must also file a Form 990-T and pay any tax required. And private foundations have certain excise taxes that they pay—the form they file is Form 990-PF. However, since Save the Chipmunks is not a private foundation and is not operating an unrelated business, it need only file Form 990."

"Okay. So should I just get my accountant to fill in the numbers? Since there is no tax due, I guess I don't really need to be concerned."

"To the contrary, Sam; you must be very diligent to see that the Form 990 is completed correctly. Although the accountant can certainly help you fill out the form, the Form 990 is too important to be left to your accountant alone.

"The reason is that, under Federal law, you must make the Forms 990 available for inspection by anyone who asks to see it. In addition, there is a website that posts all of the Forms 990 that are filed with the Internal Revenue Service.[30] Because of this, although the form was not really designed with this in mind, you should regard the Form 990 as a public relations document and make sure that it adequately and correctly reflects the operations of Save the Chipmunks. In fact, many donors now look at the Forms 990 before deciding whether to donate to an organization. Further, anyone who is not particularly friendly to your organization may use information in the Form 990 to cast your organization in a bad light. The form is also signed under penalty of perjury."

"So now I need to be a public relations expert as well?"

"Sam, you just need to make sure that the Form 990 tells your story and catches the heart of what you are trying to do. The accountant can help you with the numbers, but you need to make sure that you and the rest of the board are satisfied that if the only information about your organization someone sees is your Form 990, they will understand the purpose and goals of your organization, and what it is doing to fulfill those goals."

"Okay, I think I can do that. Is there anything else I should know about the form?"

"One item to note is that the compensation paid to the officers, directors, and key employees must be disclosed, along with the number of hours each works. As the form is required to be made publicly available, this is a matter of public record. You may want to use the address of the corporation as the address of each officer and director, rather than their personal residences, for the same reason. You need to disclose your major donors on the form, but this may be removed when the form is made available to the public unless you are a private foundation, in which case it is included in the public disclosure requirement.

"It is also recommend that you have someone knowledgeable about the form review it after you have filled it out to make sure that there are no red flags unintentionally created by any of your answers.

"A final note is that small nonprofits with gross receipts of less than $100,000 and total assets of less than $250,000 may use Form 990-EZ, which is a simplified version of the Form 990."

"I have one other question. When I mentioned to Pastor Ray that I was going to ask you about the filing requirements, he seemed to know nothing about it. Does his church have to file the Forms 990 as well?"

"No. Churches, conventions or associations of churches, and their integrated auxiliaries, as well as some other church-affiliated organizations do not have to file 990s.

---

30. See http://www.guidestar.org/.

Donors may request copies of the church's financials, but there is no legal requirement that they be furnished. Religious organizations that are not churches or integrated auxiliaries still have to file Forms 990. Some church-affiliated organizations may have decided that it is 'good business' to file Form 990 to keep their contributors happy, even if they might otherwise be exempt, but again this is not a legal requirement. Of course, we still have not talked about the unrelated business income tax; if a church has unrelated business income, it will have the same filing requirements and pay the same taxes as any other nonprofit."

Donor Substantiation Requirements

"What type of donation receipt do I have to give to my donors?" asked Sam, the next time he met with Alvin.

"Each charity must provide a receipt to contributors, whenever the amount contributed exceeds $250.

"In addition, when the contributor receives something in return for the contribution, the charity must notify each contributor of more than $75 what portion of the contribution is deductible." [31]

There is no specific language that needs to be used for the receipt. Two sample forms are included that should satisfy the receipt requirements. In a normal situation, only one of these forms is to be used.

Form I is designed to be used where there is a contribution of $250 or more to an organization, when the contributor receives nothing from the charity in exchange for the contribution, or receives only items which fall within the "insubstantial value" exception (described in Paragraph 2 of the instructions to Form I). Most donations would fall into this category.

Form II is suggested for use where a total payment in excess of $75 is made to an organization, and the donor received something that exceeded the "insubstantial value" exception mentioned above. For example, if you had a fund-raising dinner that cost $100 per ticket, and the value of the dinner was $35, then the donation allowed would be $65.

NOTE: No substantiation form is required where the transfer is for full value, with no donative intent—e.g., the purchase of an article in the thrift store, or purchase of books or videos.

---

31. The Internal Revenue Service Publication 1771 describes, in more detail, the position of the Internal Revenue Service regarding these provisions.

Form I

To: Big Donor

"Save the Chipmunks" is pleased to acknowledge your contribution on [date] of the following cash or property:[32]

"Save the Chipmunks" did not provide any goods and services in return for this contribution [OR: Only intangible religious benefits were received in return for this contribution]

Thank you for your generosity.

SAVE THE CHIPMUNKS

By:_____
      Sam Goodman, President

Date:_____

(Please retain this receipt for your tax records; your cancelled check is not sufficient.)

Instructions for Form I

Form I is suggested for use where:

1. The contribution to the charity was worth $250 or more; and
2. The charity provided no goods or services in return for the contribution; or the goods or services provided fell under the "insubstantial value" exception of Revenue Procedure 90-12 (as revised from time to time), i.e.,
   a. the fair market value of all benefits provided was not more than 2% of the contribution, or $82 (as of 2004), whichever is less; or
   b. all benefits provided fell under the low cost article limitation, i.e., the contribution is $41 or less, and the goods or services provided to the donor are token items which cost the charity not in excess of $8.20 (as of 2004) in which event the insubstantial goods and services provided need not be recorded for tax purposes.
3. If Form I is not appropriate, use Form II.

---

32. The charity need only describe the property contributed, without valuation.

Form II

SAVE THE CHIPMUNKS LETTERHEAD

To: Large Donor

Save the Chipmunks is pleased to acknowledge your contribution on [date] of the following cash or property:[33]

Save the Chipmunks provided the following goods and services in return for this contribution, with an estimated value of $_____.[34]

Only the net amount contributed (value of contribution less value of goods and services provided in return) is tax deductible as a charitable contribution.

Thank you for your generosity.

SAVE THE CHIPMUNKS
By:_____
Sam Goodman, President
*Date:*_____

(Please retain this receipt for your tax records; your cancelled check is not sufficient.)

Instructions for Form II

Form II is suggested for use where:

1. The transfer to the charity is worth more than $75; and
2. In return for the contribution, the charity provided goods and services to the donor that exceeded the "insubstantial value" described under paragraph 2 of the Instructions to Form I.
3. If Form II is not appropriate, use Form I.

---

33. The charity need only describe the property contributed, without valuation.

34. The charity is required only to make a good faith estimate of the value of the goods and services furnished in return for the contribution.

Directors' Responsibilities (Fiduciary Duties)

"Alvin, I have another question. Bill, Susan, and I got together for our regular director's meeting, and we realized that we really did not know what we were supposed to do. I know you said that we needed to establish policy, and act in the best interest of the organization. But now that the corporation is up and running, what, exactly, are our responsibilities as directors? What do directors actually do, and how do they do it?"

What Do Directors Do?

"Those are very good questions, Sam. I can give you a list of the types of issues that should be of concern to directors of a nonprofit charitable organization. However you need to realize that there is no 'one size fits all' pattern as to how you actually carry out those responsibilities and duties. This may vary, depending upon the size and structure of your nonprofit, as well as the needs of the organization and the skills that each director has. But first, we should review how a director carries out his or her responsibilities, and then what, exactly, this might entail.[35]

"We have already talked about the fact that directors have a responsibility to direct. They cannot regard the position as 'honorary,' but they must actively participate in the oversight of the organization.

"On the other hand, directors cannot become so involved in the organization that they take on the responsibilities of administration and implementation that are the duty of the officers.

"And, as you know, the directors cannot do whatever they desire with the corporation; they must make sure that the activities are in the best interests of the organization.

"*How* directors carry out their responsibilities is commonly referred to as the fiduciary duties of directors.

"Let's go through some of the basic questions that you, as directors, should ask, in determining the scope of your responsibilities and how these responsibilities should be fulfilled. We have already talked about many of these specific issues, but let's take an example and see how you would answer the questions. There may be other questions that would be relevant in specific situations, but this is a good place to start."

What are the stated purposes of the organization? A nonprofit organization must use all of its assets to advance the purposes for which the organization was formed, as set out in its articles of incorporation or bylaws (the "stated purposes"). These stated purposes are controlling over all other statements of policy issued by the organization.

"Well, our purposes are to preserve and enhance the natural habitat of chipmunks, to educate the public about chipmunks, and to take whatever steps are necessary to make sure that there will be chipmunks around for our children and their children to enjoy."

---

35. For a more detailed discussion of the responsibilities and duties of directors, see the *Guidebook for Directors of Nonprofit Corporations*, American Bar Association, Business Law Section, 2002. It is recommended that copies of this guidebook be obtained and distributed to each director of a nonprofit.

"That's a good summary, Sam. The first step each director should take is to review the organizational documents (articles, bylaws, constitution) to make sure he or she knows exactly what the purposes are. All decisions of the board should be made, and all corporate policies developed, in light of those stated purposes."

Does the transaction advance the stated purposes? In reviewing any transaction, a director must make sure that the activity primarily benefits the organization, and that any benefit to an individual is reasonable.

"After you have identified your purposes, you need to determine how any proposed activity advances these purposes. Assets may be used both for direct and indirect expenses. The cost of purchasing land that would be set aside as a natural chipmunk habitat, and the cost of putting on programs to educate the public, are direct expenses. The costs to administer the programs and solicit funds are indirect expenses. All of these costs are justified. However, expenses to fulfill another purpose, not included in the stated purposes of the organization, are not justified, even if this other purpose is more commendable."

"Like the situation we talked about earlier, of helping out the family of a friend who is terminally ill."

"That's correct, Sam. That might be a very commendable purpose, but it is not *your* purpose. So each major transaction should be reviewed to test whether it advances, either directly or indirectly, the stated purposes."

"If there is any doubt, the board should postpone the transaction until there is a consensus as to how the transaction advances the purposes."

"The minutes of the board meeting at which the matter is considered should reflect this decision process."

Does the transaction benefit a private individual? Section 501(c)(3) of the Internal Revenue Code prohibits the assets of a charitable organization from being used to benefit an individual.

"I remember. I was concerned that this would mean we would not be able to pay anyone, but you told me that is not what it meant."

"That's right. An organization can pay employees reasonable salaries and benefits without violating this provision. And an activity that advances the purpose of the organization is permitted even if an individual also receives a benefit. However, the board should determine exactly what the benefit is to the organization before approving an activity, and the minutes should reflect the benefits of the activity. If the board determines that the primary benefit is to an individual and not the organization, then the activity should not be implemented."

"If this requirement is violated and 'private benefit' or 'private inurement' is found, the organization's tax-exempt status may be lost."

"In addition to possible loss of exempt status of the organization, under what is called the 'intermediate sanctions' rules, if a person who was in a position to exercise substantial influence over the organization anytime in the past five years receives a benefit that is greater than what he provided to the organization, that person, as well as anyone approving the transaction, may face substantial penalties." (Refer to Part II, Enforcement of Laws, "Intermediate Sanctions.")

Were any promises made when the funds were raised? Funds raised for a specific purpose must be used for that specific purpose and no other.

"I remember I wanted to use some of the funds that were raised for specific purposes, to cover the general administrative costs of the organization, and you told me I could not."

"You are correct, Sam. Generally, Save the Chipmunks must use the funds for the purpose for which they were given. If that purpose becomes impossible or impractical, Save the Chipmunks should normally (a) return the funds to the donor; (b) obtain a waiver of the original purpose from the donor or the state Attorney General; or (c) obtain a court order directing disposition, before the funds are used for another purpose. State law may require certain steps to change the use of the funds."

"So we need to qualify all of our appeals so that the funds raised may be used at the discretion of the board, or we need to be prepared to use those funds in the manner represented."

"Very good, Sam."

Were any conditions placed on the donated funds? A donor may place conditions on assets he or she gives to an organization, and require that they be used for a specific purpose. The same limitation as when the funds are given in response to a specific request applies when the donor specifies the purpose.

"Save the Chipmunks may either accept the assets for the purpose specified by the donor, if it is consistent with the organization's stated purposes, or refuse to accept the assets subject to the condition. It may not accept the assets and use them for a purpose other than the purpose specified by the donor.

For example, a donor may give Save the Chipmunks a parcel of land to be set aside as a chipmunk habitat. This clearly would be consistent with the organization's purposes. However, even here the directors must be careful; if the land is not appropriate as a chipmunk habitat, the organization might want to be able to sell the land and purchase another property in a better location. Or Save the Chipmunks may determine that the cost of owning the property may be more than it can afford. In either situation, the donor should be approached to see if an agreement may be reached. For example, the donor may agree that as long as the assets are used to establish a chipmunk habitat, this would be okay, even if the property to be given is actually sold. In the second situation, perhaps the donor would be willing to provide an endowment to cover the ongoing expenses of owning and using the land. If no agreement can be reached acceptable to the nonprofit, Save the Chipmunks would be well advised to decline the contribution."

"What if we accept the property and then realize that it is not going to work for our purposes?"

"Sometimes there is a reversionary clause which states what will happen to the property if it is not used for a particular purpose. If there is no such clause, then you have the same type of situation as when you are unable to use funds for the purpose for which they were given. You either need to return the property to the donor, or obtain a waiver of the original purpose from the donor, or obtain consent of the state Attorney General or a court order, directing the disposition or change in purpose."

Does the director attend the meetings? One duty of a director is the duty of reasonable care.

"Regular attendance at meetings of the board of directors is a basic requirement of director service."[36]

To fulfill their responsibilities, directors must provide direction for the operations
of the organization. State laws generally allow for proxies for members but *not* for directors. If directors are unable to regularly attend the meetings of the board, they will
be unable to provide the necessary guidance to the corporation. Further, the directors will remain responsible for actions taken by the board, even in their absence.

Before agreeing to become a director, individuals should consider the necessary time commitment. If they are unable to make the commitment, the position
should be declined. A director who later becomes unable to attend board meetings
regularly would be well advised to resign.

Are meetings held regularly? Although directors are not normally responsible for calling meetings, a director should request that meetings be held as often
as necessary to cover the business of the organization. Meetings should be held
at least annually. Many organizations have regular board meetings quarterly, bi-
monthly, or monthly.

Most states provide that officers or two or more directors can call a board meeting.

Does the director have all the relevant facts? To make an informed decision about an action, a director must have all the relevant facts. For instance, if an
organization proposes to construct a new building, the board should review any
zoning issues, building permits, cost of construction (with bids), proposed financing arrangements, and similar factors before approving or disapproving the plan.
The board also should review any legal consequences of its decision and examine
any alternatives (such as buying an existing building) that would be more beneficial
to the organization.

A director should insist on having all of the appropriate information to review
and should review the information before making a decision.

"To satisfy the duty of care in an effective manner, a director needs to have
an adequate source of information flow. This information is generally supplied by the corporation's management and other staff. To the extent that
it is not adequate, a board or an individual director will have to determine
what additional information is needed. Needless to say, the director should
carefully read the information supplied."[37]

If for any reason sufficient information is not made appropriately available, the
director should request that action be delayed until the information is made available.

"Are you saying that we need to be construction experts before we build a
building?"

"No, Sam. As directors, you are entitled to rely upon the information furnished
to you by qualified people. However, this leads us right into the next question."

---

36. Page 19, *Guidebook for Directors of Nonprofit Corporations*, American Bar Association (2002).

37. *Id*, at page 22.

Is there any reason not to trust the information furnished? Directors are responsible for the overall activities of the organization, but generally do not manage the organization on a day-to-day basis. Consequently, they normally do not directly gather the information about the proposed activities. Unless there is some reason to suspect the reliability or competence of the individual furnishing the information, the directors may rely on the information furnished. However, directors must make whatever additional inquiries are necessary to satisfy themselves as to the validity of the information furnished if there is reasonable doubt of its reliability.

Are employment taxes being paid? If the organization has employees, income taxes and, in most cases, Social Security taxes, must be withheld and paid. If they are not withheld, the organization may still be liable for the amounts that should have been withheld. The organization, any responsible individuals, and often the directors themselves will be found to be personally liable for the amounts due even when the directors did not know these payments were not being made. This is especially true if the director had signatory authority on the bank accounts.

Is there a conflict of interest or self-dealing? Each director has a duty of complete loyalty. Directors may not use the position of director for personal profit, or to gain a personal advantage. A director cannot personally take advantage of an opportunity that belongs to the organization; nor can directors use the organization to better themselves.

For instance, if Save the Chipmunks is looking for a piece of land and Bill, one of the directors, finds a suitable parcel for a good price, Bill cannot buy the parcel and then sell it to Save the Chipmunks for a higher price. If Bill already owns a suitable parcel of land, he cannot sell it to the organization for more than its value to the organization. And, if Bill owns a parcel of land that is unsuitable, he should not attempt to sell it to the organization.

It is preferable to avoid entirely any activity that involves a conflict of interest or self-dealing (that is, any activity between the person as an individual and the person as a director; trustee). If self-dealing is unavoidable or is clearly of benefit to the organization, most states will allow it. However, the director should make sure that the conflict of interest and all relevant facts are *disclosed*, that it does not result in an unjustified advantage to the interested director (i.e., it is *fair* to the organization), and that it is *beneficial* to the organization. Even if this is done, some states will allow the transaction to be voided at the option of the organization, regardless of the results.

Corporate loans to either directors or officers are one type of self-dealing that is of particular concern. Directors who vote in favor of these loans may be liable for them in the event the loan is illegal or otherwise impermissible. Boards must check the state law under which they are incorporated before considering such loans to see if they are permitted in their state.

If a director becomes aware of an opportunity or transaction that would be of interest or benefit to the corporation he or she serves, especially if the director becomes aware of this opportunity as a result of his or her position with the organization, the director must disclose the opportunity to the corporation and permit it to take advantage of the opportunity if it so desires. If full disclosure of the opportunity is made and the corporation declines to act, the director is then free to pursue the transaction for his or her own advantage. The basis for the doctrine is the "unfairness on the particular facts" of the director taking personal advantage of an opportunity that should rightfully accrue to the corporation.

The director should make sure that state law permits the self-dealing transaction. If it does, the director should make sure that the conflict of interest is totally disclosed and that the activity is beneficial to the organization itself. Depending upon state law, failure to follow proper procedures can result in strict sanctions on directors who engage in self-dealing or conflict of interest transactions. Proper procedures may include a requirement that the interested director not participate in deliberations or vote on the matter. (See also Part II, Enforcement of Laws, Intermediate Sanctions.)

The directors should also make sure that a conflict of interest policy is adopted by the organization, and that all directors, officers and employees are aware of and agree to abide by the policy.[38] (Refer to Part II, Enforcement of Laws, Conflicts of Interest.)

Is the transaction fair to the organization? A director should determine whether an activity is fair and reasonable as far as the organization is concerned. This is normally a judgment call; however, if self-dealing is involved (see above), then the transaction must clearly be fair and reasonable.

How would an ordinarily reasonable and prudent person decide the matter? Corporate directors are expected to choose the course of action that an ordinarily reasonable and prudent person would choose in the same or similar circumstances. However, with a nonprofit corporation, that standard may differ from the standard applied in a business setting when viewed in the light of the purposes and ideals of the organization.

Therefore, the decision should not be made on the basis of what an ordinarily reasonable and prudent person in a business setting would decide, but what an ordinarily reasonable and prudent person would decide in light of the purposes and ideals of the nonprofit organization. With a religious organization, the religious beliefs and doctrine must also be taken into account.

Are there other laws that affect the particular situation? There are laws that might affect both the liability of the corporation and the directors' liability in a particular area. For example, the organization and its directors are not exempt from securities laws or from criminal laws regarding fraudulent activities. And some nonprofits have found that the anti-trust laws apply to them. This type of information should be part of the information reviewed when a particular activity is considered by the board.

How accurate are the records? Another duty of a director is the duty to account. To do this, the records of an organization must be accurate. There should be sufficient internal accounting and management procedures to assure the accuracy and control of the organization's activities and funds. As part of the record keeping, there should be no commingling of funds among directors' assets, the organization's assets, and assets belonging to any other individual or organization. Assets should be held in the name of the organization, or in the name of an individual in trust for the organization, or for a specified purpose.

---

38. A sample policy is attached as Appendix A.

"... [T]he records and accounting of the trustees should constitute a complete and a clear, accurate and distinct report and disclosure in detail of the administration of the trust, showing receipts and their sources, payments by him, and the balance remaining, to the end of distributing to the beneficiary the trust property or funds or their value, with income thereon and increments thereto, and without profits to the trustee, although allowing him compensation and reimbursement."[39]

Is the director acting honestly, in good faith, with integrity? The requirement that a director act in good faith requires directors to perform their duties honestly and with integrity. This incorporates a number of responsibilities already discussed. For instance, directors cannot rely on information they know to be false or engage in self-dealing without violating these responsibilities.

Is the transaction in the best interests of the organization? Finally, once a director has reviewed all of the issues relevant to a transaction, found the transaction to be consistent with the purposes of the organization, and reviewed all the information concerning the matter, the director should take the opportunity to look again at the entire picture. At this time, the director should make a determination that the activity or transaction is in the best interests of the organization and that there is no better alternative available at the present time.

"If you, Bill and Sue, as the directors of Save the Chipmunks, ask all of the questions listed above and act in accordance with the suggestions, it is likely that you will be performing your duties satisfactorily. However, things can still go wrong, even with the most well-intentioned directors and organization."

Matters That Should Be of Concern to the Board

"Wow. Well that gives us guidelines on how we make decisions, but it still does not address the question of what we should be deciding."

"True, Sam. And that brings us face to face with the fact that the actual decisions that your board must make will vary depending upon the activities of the organization, its size, and how much it has delegated to others. That being said, let's go over some of the basic matters that are in the scope of the directors' responsibilities (what directors do)."

Corporate governance. The structure of the corporation and the operation of the board itself needs to be reviewed periodically and revised, as necessary.

As we noted above, directors should be familiar with the articles and bylaws of the corporation. As a part of this, they need to make sure that the articles, the bylaws, and the operations of the corporation are consistent. If there is a conflict, either the documents or the operations need to be revised. It is almost always easier to make the documents conform to the operations, than it is to make the operations conform to the documents.

Directors need to have in place a method of making sure that the articles or bylaws continue to conform to law. If there are changes in the law, this may require amendments to the articles or bylaws.

---

39. 76 Am. Jur. 2d, Section 507.

Directors are generally responsible for nominating (and if the corporation has no members, electing) new directors, as well as selecting the officers. To do this adequately, there needs to be a continuing effort to determine what expertise is needed on the board, and whether there are other qualifications that need to be met (does the board need to have diversity on its board? does it need to include consumers of its services? etc.). It is also responsible to locate qualified directors, to provide board orientation of new directors, and to provide continuing board education to all directors.

There should be a procedure in place for scheduling and providing notice of board meetings, as well as for preparing and approving minutes of the board and committee meetings.

Often policies are established by board resolution, rather than being contained in the articles or bylaws. There needs to be a process for tracking the board policies. Without this it is difficult, if not impossible, for a new director to know if a policy has been developed and, if it has, whether or not it is being followed.

Approval and oversight of activities. Directors direct; officers implement. In order to fulfill their responsibilities, directors need to develop both long and short range plans for achieving the corporation's purposes. This is sometimes called "strategic planning," and a good plan will look three to five years into the future. It will then have a means to measure how effective the organization and the staff have been in working towards and carrying out these plans.

There then needs to be the development of policy. Policies may include a determination of who will be served (the constituency), the services to be provided, the framework for providing these services (such as methods of fund-raising, pursuing grant making activities, and establishing priorities among the approved goals), and developing personnel policies and procedures. The officers must then follow these policies in the implementation of the activities.

Depending upon the organization's level of sophistication, the directors may govern by defining the goals and parameters, leaving it up to the officers to determine exactly what will be done to meet the goals within the parameters set. Or the directors may establish specific guidelines for the activities to be pursued, but leave it up to the officers to determine how each activity will be carried out. Or the directors may want to approve each specific activity.

For example, the board of Joe's Home for Delinquent Boys might have a goal of establishing two new homes that will serve 30 additional children this year, but may leave it to the discretion of the officers to determine the location of each home (as long as they are within the areas served by the organization), how many staff people will be needed and what their salaries will be (as long as they are within the guidelines for numbers of children per staff member and the salaries fall within the ranges established for each job position). Or, the directors may require the officers to return for approval of each new home location, the number of children it will serve, and also for approval of the new staff members and their salaries.

The more the directors can establish guidelines and parameters, trusting the officers to carry out their duties without constant oversight, the more effective and efficient both the directors and the staff will be. Generally this does not happen unless and until the staff have demonstrated a level of competence that assures the directors that their trust is not misplaced. However, the directors should not usurp the duties of the officers. They need to remember that the directors direct; the officers implement.

In addition to development and periodic review of policies and approving major activities of the corporation, the Board will generally approve all contracts for services, grants, and funding proposals, and all loans and bank accounts (including the signers). They are ultimately responsible to evaluate risk exposure and to determine what insurance is necessary for the corporation, the Board, and the individual directors. They should have in place a structure to assure quality control. They should approve transfers of real property, property and equipment leases, major corporate contracts, and any other significant corporate activities.

Financial oversight. One of the more important areas of oversight is in the financial arena. There are several parts to this.

The first area of oversight is determining the method of handling money and approving expenditures. As with the oversight of activities, this may be done on several different levels. For example, the directors may establish goals and parameters setting forth the activities to be pursued, and requiring at the same time that the organization must finish the year with a balanced budget, while leaving it up to the officers to determine exactly where the money will come from and how it will be allocated between the various activities. Or, the directors may approve certain activities and adopt a budget that gives a certain amount of discretion within categories; the officers are then authorized to spend up to the amounts budgeted, but must come back to the board for additional approval for increased expenditures if the amounts exceed the budgeted amounts, even if funds have been raised, sufficient to pay for the increase. Or (not recommended), the directors may approve each expenditure as it arises.

It is not enough to direct the spending of the funds. There must be in place some method to review the financial picture of the organization on a regular basis to make sure that the organization is meeting its financial goals and to assure that the assets of the organization continue to be used to benefit the exempt purpose of the organization and not for the benefit of a nonexempt person.

The most common method used by nonprofits to review and approve expenditures is to establish a budget, which is generally prepared by staff and approved by the Board. The Board then receives periodic financial statements showing income and expenses with year to date comparisons to the approved budget and (preferably) the prior year at the same period.

In addition to directing the spending of the money, directors of nonprofits need to assure that the money is there to spend. The level of involvement with fund-raising varies significantly among nonprofits. The directors of nonprofits that are funded almost exclusively by government contracts, or that are private foundations and do little if any solicitation of funds from outside third parties, may have virtually no involvement with fund-raising. Other nonprofits that are publicly supported may rely on their directors to contact significant donors. Many significant gifts are made in response to requests by individuals with whom the contributor has a pre-existing relationship. In any event, directors need to be aware of restrictions on any funds raised and see that these restrictions are met. They should also be aware of and approve all methods of solicitation.

The second area of financial oversight involves hiring and overseeing the auditor. Not all nonprofits are required to be audited, and a small nonprofit may not be able to afford an audit. However, the trend is to require audits. Some boards find an audit to be appropriate, and sometimes a funding source will require an audit.

Every nonprofit also needs to keep track of what their state legislature is doing in this area. Because of recent scandals, Congress adopted new rules applicable to public companies (the Sarbanes-Oxley Act of 2002). Some states are considering whether any of these rules should be applied to nonprofits, and proposals have been made to require audits of nonprofits over a certain size. In January of 2003, New York's Attorney General, Eliot Spitzer, proposed a version of the federal law to be applicable to New York's nonprofits. California adopted a requirement, effective January 1, 2005, that requires most nonprofits with annual income of $1,000,000 or more to have an annual audit, to furnish this audit to the Attorney General, and to make the audit available to the general public in the same manner as the Form 990 (see below).

An audit is prepared by an independent certified public accountant who has no other (or very restricted) connection with the organization. The auditor should be hired by the board (or by an audit committee) and answer to the board, rather than to the staff. Although the auditor will work with the staff to complete the audit, it should be clear that the board hired the auditor, and it is the board to whom the auditor is accountable. After the audit is completed, either the entire board or an audit committee should meet with the auditor for a closing interview. All directors should receive a copy of the audit and any management letters and have a chance to raise any questions they may have.

Regulatory filings; public relations. The directors need to make sure that the required filings are made by the organization. Along with this, because these filings are generally matters of public record, the directors should make sure the forms are completed in a manner that will inform the public, as well as providing the required information to the government. Because these forms are matters of public record, it is advisable for the directors to have reviewed and be familiar with the information contained therein.

Form 1023. Form 1023, Application for Recognition of Exemption, as filed with the Internal Revenue Service, including all correspondence between the IRS and the organization, culminating in the issuance by the IRS of an exempt determination letter, is one of the first filings to be made by the organization. If the application was filed before July 15, 1987, and the organization did not have a copy of the application on that date, it does not have to be made available for inspection by the public. If the filing was made after July 15, 1987, or if the organization had a copy of the application on that date, the Form 1023 is required to be made available to anyone who requests to see it. If the application is required to be made available, that you cannot find it is not an excuse; you must find the application (a copy may be requested from the IRS).

Form 1023 should be reviewed periodically to make sure there has been no change in purpose. If there is a change in the articles or bylaws, especially to the purpose clause, or if new activities have been added, it is appropriate to notify the IRS of the change. This can be done either by filing directly with the IRS, or by providing such information along with the organization's annual Form 990.

Form 990. Form 990 is the annual information return filed with the Internal Revenue Service. Some states require that this form also be filed with them. The last three years of Forms 990 are also required to be made available to the general public for inspection (or copies furnished at a nominal cost).

It should be noted that all Forms 990 that are filed with the Internal Revenue Service, can also be found online at http://www.guidestar.org. Guidestar will also post additional information to its website if it is provided by the organization. For example, some organizations provide Guidestar with audited financials and other information. It is recommended that every organization look at the Guidestar site to see what information is included about their organization, to see if the information is correct, and if additional information should be provided. As this website is readily available, many potential contributors, along with those who might be critical of the organization, go directly to Guidestar to obtain information about the organization. Because of this, it is recommended that when a Form 990 is completed, care be given to ensure that anyone reviewing the form can readily determine the activities and purpose of the organization, and why it is and should remain exempt.

State filings. Some states require informational returns similar to the Form 990 to be filed with the state taxing authority.

Annual or bi-annual informational filings are also generally required by the state of incorporation, and by other states in which the organization is qualified to do business, often by the Secretary of State. These informational filings provide information such as the registered agent or agent for service of process, the organization's registered address, and the principal officers of the organization.

Some states may require additional filings with the state charitable office (often the Attorney General). For example, the State of California requires that an annual form that provides information about the activities of the organization be filed, along with the Federal Form 990. States may also post information about charities (as well as their filing requirements) on the web.

Form 990-T. If the organization engages in an unrelated business that results in taxable income of $1,000 or more, a Form 990-T must be filed with the IRS. Some states again require corresponding filings to be made with the state taxing authority.

Legislative activity. If the organization engages in legislative lobbying, additional filings, both on a federal and a state level, may be required.

Other information made public. In addition to the information contained in the required filings, many nonprofits choose to make information directly available to the community. For example, press releases may be issued when a particularly notable activity occurs.

What many organizations are not ready for is how to deal with the media when a crisis occurs. It is always better to have thought about this beforehand, including appointing a spokesperson, rather than waiting until disaster strikes. Every officer and director, as well as all employees should know who the spokesperson is and be instructed to refer any inquiries to that person, rather than attempting to answer questions themselves. This will assure that a consistent and complete answer will be provided, and will also assure that the officers and directors will not inadvertently provide confidential or sensitive information, the disclosure of which might violate the duty of care or the duty of loyalty.

Employee or volunteer oversight. One of the main responsibilities of the board of directors is to hire and evaluate the Executive Director or CEO. The directors or a committee of the Board should evaluate the Executive Director or CEO annually, based on objective criteria to the highest degree possible.

All other employees report to the Executive Director or CEO. Although other employees may work with the board (for example, the chief financial officer may be an advisor to the Finance Committee), this is a convenience, and it should not be misinterpreted as a change the chain of command.

Having said that, there are several areas involving other employees with which the board may be involved. First, because of recent changes in the law, although the CFO reports to the CEO, the board will want to make sure that it has approved the CFO's salary as being reasonable (Refer to Part II, Enforcement of Laws, Intermediate Sanctions).

Secondly, the board may often adopt a policy whereby employee appeals, disputes, and complaints (particularly complaints of harassment or discrimination involving management personnel) that cannot be resolved at a staff level are referred to the board for resolution. This provides the board with an opportunity to resolve a dispute prior to a lawsuit being brought.

Finally, the board may adopt a personnel manual and determine what benefits (such as pension benefits, vacation time, sick leave, etc.) will be offered to employees. Note that if any personnel policies are adopted, they must be followed. Failure to do so may increase the possibility of a successful lawsuit against the organization or its officers and directors.

Bringing a Director "Up to Speed"

Because directors have significant responsibilities and duties, many of which they cannot adequately fulfill without having the basic information about the organization, it is recommended that new directors receive basic information about the organization. Additionally, it is recommended that all directors regularly review the organization and their part in it, perhaps at a board retreat. Refer to Chapter 12, *Guidebook for Directors of Nonprofit Corporations*,[40] for more specific suggestions on how to do this.

Observing Corporate Formalities

Clearly the duties of directors are significant. In addition to actually fulfilling its responsibilities, the board needs to create a record of its decisions. This record should document the fact that decisions of directors were made after due consideration of the pertinent factors. The greatest liability and exposure occurs, not when a wrong decision was made after due consideration, but when no decision was made at all, was made without due consideration, or was not properly documented. If proper documentation exists of the decision made (for example, in the minutes of the board meetings), a court is unlikely to second guess the decision of the board.

---

40. *Guidebook for Directors of Nonprofit Corporations*, 2nd Edition, American Bar Association, Business Law Section, 2002.

A corporation is an entity, separate from the individuals involved with it. To receive all of the benefits associated with doing business in the corporate form, it is important for the directors, officers, and members to demonstrate that the actions in which they participated were performed by and on behalf of the corporate entity. That corporate actions were intended is most commonly demonstrated by a complete set of corporate minutes, board resolutions, and contracts executed in the name of the corporation by its duly authorized agents. If verification of corporate action cannot be made because records have been poorly maintained or are nonexistent, it may be possible for persons dealing with directors, officers, or members to hold them personally liable. This is commonly referred to as "piercing the corporate veil."

Poor record keeping can also jeopardize a nonprofit corporation's tax-exempt status, since the IRS and the state taxing authorities can demand proof that the corporation is operating in a manner consistent with its exempt classification.

Action taken at formal meetings or by written consent. Since directors are agents acting on behalf of the corporation, it is very important that their actions be taken in accordance with all legal requirements and that their actions be properly documented. Directors are only authorized to take action in two ways, namely, at a properly noticed meeting at which a quorum is present, or by written consent (most states require written consent to be unanimous—e.g., signed by all of the directors; some states permit majority written consent).

Notice of meetings should be given in the manner required by the corporate bylaws and the state corporation law. If a quorum of the board fails to appear at a meeting, no valid action can be taken, other than to adjourn the meeting.

If notice is given, a copy of the notice should be included with the minutes of the board meeting and filed, along with the minutes, in the corporate minute book. If the meeting is held without notice, there should be a waiver of notice and consent to holding of the meeting, signed by any director who did not participate in the meeting. If any director objects to lack of notice, the meeting cannot be held until proper notice is given.

There is often debate regarding the degree of detail that should be reflected in the minutes of corporate proceedings. Minutes should be a record of what was done, not what was said. In other words, minutes need not (and probably should not) be a verbatim transcript of every word that was spoken at the meeting. Instead, minutes should accurately document the actions that were approved at the meeting. Minutes can also present a summary description of any preliminary discussion, in advance of formal action, which may be necessary to understand the nature and intent of the approved course of action. A good question to ask is whether you would understand what occurred at the meeting if you were not in attendance and only had an opportunity to read the minutes.

It should also be noted that, especially in matters involving conflicts of interest or approval of compensation matters, more complete documentation may be necessary (Refer to Part II, Enforcement of Laws, Intermediate Sanctions).

Another issue that is often debated is the merits of making audio or video recordings of Board meetings. Recording meetings is generally inadvisable because the recording cannot serve as the official record of the proceedings, and yet the tape will be available, with all of its discord and errors in syntax, for use in the context of litigation proceedings. If the corporate secretary desires to tape record the proceedings of the Board for purposes of assuring accuracy in the preparation of written minutes, the corporation should adopt a policy that calls for erasure of the tape once the written minutes have been read and approved.

If a director disagrees with the actions approved by the Board majority, the director has a right to demand that his or her dissent be noted in the minutes. Affirmative disapproval of actions could protect the dissenting director from personal liability in the event that the majority's actions result in liability.

Absence of Personal Liability (The "Business Judgment Rule")

"So if we do all of this, does this mean that we won't be liable if something goes wrong? For instance, our board recently approved establishing trails through the chipmunk preserve, so that people can visit. What if someone gets hurt?"

With the exception, perhaps, of liability for "conflict of interest transactions," if a director performs his or her duties in accordance with the standards discussed above,[41] the director is normally not liable for any action taken or not taken as a director. This exemption, which is commonly referred to as the "business judgment rule," applies even when the director's actions or omissions exceed or defeat the corporation's purpose.

The business judgment rule is rooted in the idea that directors should be entitled to (and in order to properly manage an enterprise must) exercise a broad range of discretion in issues of corporate management and should not be subjected to hindsight assessments of their decisions by the courts. The rule originated in the context of business corporations where shareholders often expect management to take risks in order to maximize profits. Although profit seeking is generally absent from the nonprofit, the justifications for the rule are no less compelling for directors of nonprofit corporations, since the element of risk taking and the need for the organization to operate in a "business-like fashion" in order to continue in operation are present. Therefore, the concept that directors' decisions should not be second-guessed without a substantial basis for doing so remains relevant to nonprofits. Frequently, it will not be obvious which of several alternative decisions will turn out to best further the corporation's mission.

Exception for tortious conduct. Despite the business judgment rule, even if directors do everything correctly, they may be liable. For example, in California, the Supreme Court found that the business judgment rule is not a bar to individual director liability if a director participates in harmful conduct, *even if the director is acting in his or her official capacity.* The Supreme Court found that a director could be individually liable if: (a) the director specifically authorized, directed, or participated in the harmful conduct; or (b) the director knew or should have known that a condition under the board's control was hazardous and could cause injury and

---

41. Section 8.30 of the Revised Model Nonprofit Corporation Act

yet the director negligently failed to take action to avoid the harm; and (c) an ordinarily prudent person, possessing the same knowledge as the director, would have acted differently. The court also held that any director who did not vote in favor of the action that caused the injury would have a defense to personal liability.[42]

Many state legislatures have attempted to overrule court decisions and to extend some measure of protection to directors of nonprofit corporations. Many of these protections require that the directors be volunteers in order to be effective; some require that there be insurance, or that there be a provision included in the corporation's articles before the state statute will be effective. It is unclear whether any of these statutes will actually prove to be effective in limiting the liability of directors.

"So if we can be sued even if we do everything correctly, what protection do we have?"

"That is where indemnification and directors and officers liability insurance ("D and O Insurance") come in. I would not serve on the board of a nonprofit that did not have directors and officers liability insurance. Even if you are ultimately found to have no liability, the cost of the defense is likely to be significant. Insurance will cover these costs of defense as well as providing protection in the event the board is found to have done something for which they are liable."

"Who should I call?"

"There are a number of regular insurance companies that offer D and O insurance. In addition, nonprofit organizations have been formed for the purpose of providing affordable insurance to nonprofits in some states."[43]

ENFORCEMENT OF LAWS

State Jurisdiction (Attorney General)

Because the beneficiaries of any charitable enterprise are never specifically defined individuals, but rather are the purposes that advance the public good or that provide benefits to a significant segment of the general public, often no single person has sufficient economic interest to monitor the organization's activities.

Even if an individual had the necessary interest and financial ability to oversee the charitable activities of an organization, most laws do not give individuals the right to sue a charity to require it to adhere to and carry out its charitable purpose.

Thus, the charitable enforcement division of a state, commonly the Attorney General's office, as guardian of the public good, is given broad supervisory authority to assure that this "charitable trust" is carried out, and that organizations comply with other applicable laws.

Many states require that nonprofit exempt organizations file regular reports with the state's Attorney General. This will differ from state to state, as will the level of enforcement activity. In states such as New York, Massachusetts, Pennsylvania, and California, the Attorney General has an active enforcement division.

---

42. See Frances T. v. Village Green Owner Assn., 42 Cal.3d 490, 509-511 (1986).
43. See http://www.insurancefornonprofits.org and also http://www.nonprofitrisk.org.

Federal Jurisdiction

The principal federal agency with responsibility over nonprofit organizations is the Internal Revenue Service. This arises out of the Internal Revenue Code provisions setting forth when an organization is exempt from taxation, and when it might be subject to taxation.

IRS Audits

"By the way, Sam, how is your brother-in-law Joe, doing? I have not heard from him in a while."

"He is up to his eyeballs in alligators right now. The IRS has been auditing his organization and accusing him of all sorts of things. The IRS seems to think that he has been running the organization for his own benefit, even though it is obvious that he is providing an extremely valuable benefit for the children his organization is serving. I've never seen such a change in a child before I watched how he worked with children that no one else would touch."

"He's not trying to represent himself, is he? If he is, that is just asking for trouble. As you, yourself, have already found out, the IRS speaks a different language than the rest of us. The fact that the nonprofit is doing good things does not mean that you can overlook any irregularities that occur in doing so. And if Joe is trying to explain his position to the IRS personally, without understanding the way that the IRS may be interpreting his statements, he may be digging his pit even deeper. Just because he is getting good results with his operations does not mean that he has not violated some law or engaged in some questionable activity."

Even apart from addressing the specific legal issues he is facing in the IRS audit, there are several procedural steps that Joe or his representative should try to take:

1. As much as possible, keep the audit process in-house. If the agent is talking with Joe rather than to outside entities, Joe will be able to answer any questions and provide any necessary background or backup documentation to address issues that arise. In addition, Joe will want to know everything the IRS knows about his organization, which is difficult if the IRS is obtaining its information from another source. Joe should understand, of course, that the IRS may well have already obtained information from other sources, and that if Joe does not produce the same information, the IRS may consider this to be an attempt to hide some wrongdoing.

2. Joe needs to be doing his own audit of the organization, so that he can identify the potential issues on which the IRS may focus. He should look, not only for possible issues against the organization, but also issues in its favor. These will be points that Joe can use as bargaining tools, if necessary. However, Joe should not wait until the agent has completed the audit to bring them to the attention of the auditor; if he does, he may trigger another round of reviews. Along with this, Joe should not assume that the IRS understands how his organization works; part of the process of the audit is educating the IRS agent about the organization, its activities, and how it keeps its records.

3. Determine who will work with the agent. This is crucial. Joe needs to limit who works with the agent as much as possible, so as to maintain control over the process. As part of this, Joe needs to keep track of everyone the agent talks to and what they say, along with the documents examined. This, again, is not done to keep information from the IRS, but keep the corporation informed of the status of the investigation, and to make sure that the person communicating with the IRS understands how the organization works and can answer questions about the organization.

4. Be honest with the IRS.

5. If you are going to withhold documents because they are privileged, let the IRS know what you are withholding and why.

6. If necessary, reconcile the books to the Form 990 and, if filed, the Form 990-T. If Joe does not do this, then the agent will—and he or she may spend time examining other items that would not otherwise be reviewed. Note that many audits are caused by poorly prepared 990s.

7. Document everything the agent asks for, and the organization's response to the request. If the request seems overly broad, see if you can work with the agent to narrow it down to what the agent really wants. By keeping track of what the agent is requesting and reviewing the documents furnished, it may be possible to determine the areas of concern. In this way you will be able to better address the issues and even to voluntarily furnish additional documents, when these are necessary for the agent to fully understand the position of the organization.

8. Be aware that requests for information having nothing to do with the organization's liability are usually made by agents going after a third party. There is nothing Joe can or should do to limit this review, as an agent can always make a case for needing the information requested.

9. Agents can resolve issues based on factual disputes; they have much less authority to settle issues that involve an interpretation of law. If the organization reaches a settlement with the agent, make sure the settlement is based on the facts, and not on legal issues.

"I will make sure Joe calls you right away," Sam replies.

Private Inurement, Private Benefit, and Intermediate Sanctions

True to his word, Sam called Joe immediately after leaving Alvin's office. Joe, having been sufficiently berated by Sam, called to set up an appointment with Alvin for the following day. Alvin asked Joe to bring copies of all correspondence he had received so far from the IRS, what he had furnished to them, and anything else he had that might show what the government thought was the problem.

"Hi, Joe. I heard you were having a problem with the IRS. What's going on?"

"Well, you remember I mentioned that we have an Auxiliary that had accumulated a relatively large reserve? I was interested in seeing that at least some of it was used to advance our purposes now, rather than keeping it all invested for the future."

"I remember. What happened?"

"When I talked to the board of the Auxiliary, they agreed that it was not necessary to keep all of the funds in reserve and transferred $100,000 to Joe's Home for Delinquent Boys. When my board looked at it, they decided that I should get a bonus of $10,000."

"Joe, are you on the board?"

"Well, of course. But I did not vote on the bonus."

"That's good. Did you leave the room when the board discussed the matter?"

"No. Should I have?"

"It would have been a good idea, even if it may not be legally required. However, that brings up another issue. Does your corporation have a conflict of interest policy that outlines how potential conflicts are handled? For example, did you participate in the discussion about the bonus?"

"We have a general policy that directors refrain from voting when a conflict is present, but I am not aware that we have any other requirements. Are you telling me that we should develop a more comprehensive policy?"

"I would certainly recommend that your organization do so, Joe. So is this what the IRS is challenging?"

"It is one of the points. We have another problem as well. I had been pushing the board to have a retreat to do some serious long-range planning. Since we now had uncommitted funds, the board decided that we should go ahead and have the board retreat, which we had on a cruise to Mexico. Each board member brought their spouse, and we made it into a retreat-weekend vacation for the families. It seemed like a good idea, since we have sometimes had problems getting all of the directors to show up for extra meetings. Now the IRS is claiming that both my bonus and the funds spent on the retreat are what they call an 'excess benefit'; they are demanding that both I and the board personally repay the funds, and they are talking about assessing major penalties. They are also auditing our books for the last three years to see what else we may have done that they can tax us for. What did we do wrong, and what should we do now? I thought that board retreats were good."

"Board retreats are good. But expenses incurred need to be reasonable and related to the organization's purpose. So we have both conflicts of interest and intermediate sanctions issues that we need to review. Anything else?"

"No, I think that's it."

"Okay. Let's begin with a review of the law first, and then let's figure out what you did wrong and what we can do to correct it."

Basis for Revocation of Exemption

Probably the most common reason today for a charity to have its exempt status revoked is "private benefit" or "private inurement," where an activity of the charity results in a nonexempt person (either an individual or an entity) receiving a benefit greater than the value received by the charity from the person. This is also the area that appears to make it to the front page of the newspaper most quickly. Inurement has also been the principal concern raised by Congress as a reason for increased regulation of exempt organizations.

As a result, the compensation paid or benefits accruing to executives, insiders, directors, and officers, should be carefully reviewed.

The determination of reasonableness of compensation, as well as what benefits are taxable to the individual, are the same for exempt organizations as they are for businesses.

Any private benefit received by an individual, in addition to being reasonable, must also be incidental to the benefits received by the organization.

Conflicts of Interest

When a director is making a decision on behalf of the corporation, the director must be looking out for the corporation's best interests, rather than his or her own. When a decision could benefit or harm the director personally, then the director is considered to have a conflict of interest. Limiting and regulating conflicts of interest is often addressed in the state law.

This has also become a particular concern to the IRS, especially making sure that the assets of the charity are used to benefit its charitable purpose, rather than principally benefiting a private individual. One way to assuage the IRS's concerns is to adopt a conflict of interest policy. The presence of a conflicts of interest policy will allow the board to make decisions in an objective manner without undue influence from interested persons. This will help to assure that the organization fulfills its charitable purposes, and that compensation paid is reasonable.[44]

Although generally not required to be in the bylaws, either by state law or the Internal Revenue Code, the IRS "favorably views organizations having policy statements in their bylaws which clearly identify situations where a conflict might arise."[45]

"What should be in such a policy?"

"That's a good question, Joe. A well-written policy will take into account both the state law and the IRS recommendations. It should also take into account the purposes of the organization. For example, an art museum may want to include provisions concerning the acquisition of artwork in which the museum has an interest. This type of provision would be of little use to a school. However, at a minimum, the IRS would like to see a conflict of interest policy require:

1. Full disclosure by the interested party of the potential conflict.
2. Procedures to determine if the interest is likely to result in an actual conflict (for example, the art museum could decide it is not interested in a particular acquisition).
3. Procedures to be followed when the board considers and votes on matters that may involve conflicts of interest, such as requiring the interested person to leave the meeting during the discussion of and the vote on the transaction involving the conflict; perhaps investigating alternatives that would not involve a conflict; requiring a majority of the disinterested directors to de-

---

44. See the *FY 1997 Exempt Organizations CPE Technical Instruction Program Textbook*, Chapter C,"Community Board and Conflicts of Interest Policy," pp. 18-19.

45. *FY 1996 CPE Textbook Chapter P,* pp. 386-7.

termine that the transaction is in the organization's best interests, will be entered into for its own benefit, is fair and reasonable to the organization, and is the most advantageous choice; and determining what steps are appropriate to correct a situation where the interested person violates the conflicts of interest policy.

4. Procedures to document in the board minutes, the conflict, what steps were taken to assure that the procedures set forth in item 3 were followed, and who voted for the transaction.

5. Procedures to make sure that all directors and officers are aware of the policy and agree to follow it.[46]

"Even apart from application of the policy to specific potential conflict situations, the nonprofit should periodically review its activities to make sure it is operating in a manner consistent with accomplishing its charitable purpose and that does not result in private inurement or impermissible private benefit."

"Can you give us an example of a conflict of interest policy that we can use in developing our own policy?"

"Sure, Joe. I would be happy to do so. Even if it does not help directly with the current situation, if the IRS is convinced you are trying to operate correctly, this may help in our negotiations."[47]

Intermediate Sanctions

"This brings us to the next area of law, which may be the most important change in the last 30 years in the area of nonprofit law—what is commonly referred to as 'intermediate sanctions.'"

"Yeah—you and the IRS agent both referred to intermediate sanctions, but I'm not sure what it means."

"In the past, if an exempt organization operated to benefit a private person, the only remedy the IRS had was to revoke the exempt status of the organization. This often did not penalize the wrongdoers, but actually hurt the beneficiaries who no longer could receive services from the organization whose tax exempt status was now revoked. So on July 30, 1996, Congress adopted a law that provides an alternative, or an 'intermediate step' to revocation of the exempt status of an organization.[48]

"The Internal Revenue Service may now impose penalties on certain persons who improperly benefit from transactions with an exempt organization. The penalty is imposed directly on the person(s) who benefit from the transaction, rather than the organization.

"The basic concept is that if someone who is, or within the past five years has been, in a position to substantially influence the organization (that would include you, Joe) receives an 'excess benefit'—i.e., more than the person is entitled to, based on what he or she provides to the organization—that person must repay the excess benefit (plus interest) along with a penalty of 25% of the excess benefit. In

---

46. *FY 1997 CPE Textbook Chapter C*, p. 21-23.
47. See Appendix A for a draft of a conflict of interest policy.
48. See the Taxpayer Bill of Rights 2, which added section 4958 to the Internal Revenue Code.

addition, if the excess benefit (plus interest) is not repaid in a timely manner, the IRS may impose an additional 200% penalty. Further, anyone who approved the benefit, even if the approving persondid not receive a dime, is subject to a penalty of 10% of the benefit, up to $10,000 per transaction."

"So, if my $10,000 bonus is found to be an excess benefit, I will have to repay the entire bonus?"

"Plus interest."

"And I will also have to pay a penalty of $2,500?"

"Unless the penalty is waived."

"And the board will have to pay a penalty of $1,000?"

"That's right."

"And if I don't have $12,500 to repay immediately, the IRS will charge me $20,000?"

"Yes. And that $20,000 would be in addition to the $12,500 payable by you and the $1,000 payable by the board."

Joe took a deep breath.

"So this whole thing is more serious than I realized. I had no idea they had that power."

"You are not the only one, Joe. Even though the IRS has tried to make this public, many people working with exempt organizations are still not aware of this law. And my summary above is very simplistic; there has been at least one entire book written only on the subject of intermediate sanctions."[49]

"You said I was, what do you call it? Someone with substantial influence?"

"Yes. Anyone with substantial influence is what is called a 'disqualified person.' You, as the Chief Executive Officer, are automatically a disqualified person, as is your Chief Financial Officer and your board, along with your relatives. If you own more than 35% of a company, that company will also be disqualified.

"Other people may be found to be disqualified based on facts and circumstances—for instance, even if you were not an officer or director, you might be a disqualified person because you were the founder of the organization.

"It should be noted that the other side also applies: If someone is not disqualified, they will not be subject to the intermediate sanctions, even if the amount they are paid is clearly unreasonable, although there may be other ways of going after them."

"If I am a disqualified person, does that mean that anything I get will be subject to intermediate sanctions?"

"You can still be paid. But your compensation, including many of your benefits, must be found to be reasonable. If a part of your compensation is determined to be more than what is reasonable, then the intermediate sanctions penalties go into effect."

"But am I at risk of the IRS finding that ANYTHING I make is unreasonable?"

Safe Harbor. "There are steps you can take, Joe, so that your compensation fits into what is sometimes called a 'safe harbor.' This safe harbor provides that if

---

49. See Bruce Hopkins, *The Law of Intermediate Sanctions*, 2003, John Wiley & Sons, Inc.

certain requirements are met, then the burden switches from you to prove that your compensation is reasonable, to the IRS to prove that the compensation is unreasonable. The safe harbor requires three steps:

1. Approval by a Disinterested Board. A board or a committee of the board that is composed entirely of people who are unrelated to you and not subject to your control must approve the arrangement. Since you are a director, you must not participate in the decision regarding your salary (although you may participate in decisions about other matters). You may meet with other directors to answer questions, but should recuse yourself from the rest of the discussion so that you are not present during the debate and voting on the transaction or compensation arrangement. For the safe harbor to be available, the decision by the disinterested board or committee must be made at or before the payment is made.

2. Based on Independent Valuation. The board or committee must obtain and rely upon outside objective information to determine that an arrangement is reasonable. For example, you might look at compensation paid by similar organizations (both taxable and nontaxable) for similar positions, independent compensation surveys compiled by independent firms, actual written offers to the disqualified person from similar institutions, and independent appraisals of any property that is the subject of the transaction. If your organization has annual gross receipts of less than $1 million, it may rely upon data of compensation paid by five comparable organizations in the same or similar communities for similar services. It is clear that you can look at what is paid by for-profit entities as well as by nonprofits, in order to determine what is reasonable.

3. Adequate Documentation. The decision must be adequately documented, with the basis for determining reasonableness clearly defined. The minutes should set forth: a) the terms of the transaction and the date it was approved; b) the directors present during the debate, and who voted; c) the comparability data obtained and relied upon, and how it was obtained; and d) any actions taken concerning the transaction by any director who had a conflict of interest (e.g., they recused themselves from the meeting). If the board determines that reasonable compensation at fair market value is actually higher or lower than the comparables obtained, the basis for this determination must be recorded. Minutes of the meeting must be prepared by the next meeting of the board, and they must be reviewed and approved by the board as being reasonably accurate and complete within a reasonable time thereafter.

"If these steps are taken, then to prevail, the IRS will have to furnish additional information to show that the compensation was not reasonable, or that the transfer was not at fair market value."

"But this does not apply to my current situation, since we did not follow a salary survey."

"Correct. For your current situation, it is up to us to prove that your total compensation package, including this bonus, was reasonable."

"Okay, now back to my board. You said they could be liable even if they didn't receive any money themselves."

"The term the law uses for a person who may have this type of liability is *organization manager*. An organization manager is any officer, director, trustee, or person having similar powers or responsibilities, regardless of his or her title. A person is an officer if specifically so designated under the articles or bylaws of the organization, or if he or she regularly exercises general authority to make administrative or policy decisions for the organization. If a person only makes recommendations, but cannot implement decisions without approval of a superior, that person is not an officer. An *organization manager* who *participates* in an excess benefit transaction, *knowing* that it is such a transaction, is liable for penalties unless the participation was not *willful*, and was due to *reasonable cause*."

"So if they have relied upon a salary survey, they wouldn't be liable?"

"If that reliance was reasonable (if they had no reason to distrust the information), then you are correct, they probably would not have the liability."

"Does this apply to all nonprofits? I recently agreed to serve on the board of my local YMCA. Do I have potential liability because of this?"

"Yes, Joe. This law applies to virtually all 501(c)(3) and 501(c)(4) organizations other than private foundations (which are already subject to their own excise tax law)."

Benefits to board. "I think I am going to have to call a special board meeting to talk about all of this. I don't think anyone on our board is aware of the potential liability."

"Well, before you do that, let's talk about that board retreat you had."

"Oh, yes, our cruise to Mexico."

"How much did the cruise cost, per person?"

"I don't remember exact figures, but I think it was $1250, per couple."

"Which means that the benefit to each spouse was $625."

"Right. But I must interject here that the value that is provided by each director is far in excess of the value of the cruise. Certainly if we look at it from the basis of reasonable compensation, there should not be a question of the reasonableness."

"Joe, when did you take the cruise?"

"Near the end of last year."

"Did you report the value of the cruise—or at least that portion paid for each spouse—as compensation to each director?"

"Of course not. They weren't being paid."

"The problem, Joe, is that if there was compensation paid, even if it would otherwise be reasonable, and that compensation was not reported when it should have been, it will be automatically deemed to be an excess benefit. Although you might be able to argue that the amount paid for the directors to attend the retreat was a reasonable business expense to the nonprofit, it has been clearly established that spousal travel is not deductible as a business expense. Therefore, the amount of compensation received by each director that should have been reported was the $625 paid for each spouse. Any amount of nonemployee compensation over $600 must be reported on a Form 1099. Because you did not do this, it ends up falling into the excess benefit category."

"So what should we do?"

"My recommendation would be that each director immediately reimburse the corporation for the $625 spousal travel. At this point, the IRS is most concerned about getting the organizations into compliance. If you do this, you might even get them to waive the penalties, although this is not certain."

"Okay. My board is not going to want to hear this. Any other good news you have for me?"

"I think that's it for now, Joe. Let me know if you have any other questions, or if I can help explain any of this to your board."[50]

Legal Protection for Directors

"I have another question," said Sam at his next meeting with Alvin.

"Well, Sam, I figured that was why you were here. What can I do for you today?"

"I told my board that we needed to get directors and officers liability insurance, and Bill, who is serving as the treasurer, said that he did not think it was necessary. He said that he read an article that mentioned a federal law that protects volunteers, and that most states have laws that protect volunteers as well. He did not think it was worth spending the money on insurance if we were already protected. The other director agreed with him. I know you thought insurance was important, so I figured you would know if he was correct."

Volunteer Protection Laws

"Bill is correct that there are such laws. He is incorrect if he thinks that those laws are adequate to protect you from all potential liability.

"The Volunteer Protection Act of 1997 was enacted into law by the United States Congress (111 Stat. 218). As with similar state laws, the purpose of this Act is to limit lawsuits against volunteers serving nonprofit organizations and governmental agencies. The Act was enacted in response to volunteers withdrawing from service to nonprofit organizations because of concerns about possible liability. By limiting lawsuits against such volunteers, it was thought that the number of volunteers would increase, thus promoting the ability of nonprofit organizations and governmental entities to provide services at a reasonable cost.

"The Act provides that, if a volunteer meets certain criteria, he or she has a complete defense to an action and has no liability. Even when the volunteer does not meet the criteria, he or she may still have some protection against awards of noneconomic and punitive damages, as long as the volunteer has not engaged in specific types of prohibited conduct.

"The intention of this law is laudable. Unfortunately, the Act is unlikely to provide significant protection for volunteers. Any statutory scheme that merely limits liability will not decrease lawsuits. Only to the degree that a statute *prohibits* suits against volunteers and transfers all liability for the volunteer's conduct to the or-

---

50. For further information about intermediate sanctions, see http://www.runquist.com/article_intermed-sancts.htm. Also see Bruce Hopkins, *The Law of Intermediate Sanctions*, 2003, John Wiley & Sons, Inc.

ganization will lawsuits against volunteers be avoided. It will *not* shield volunteers from the time, expense, and aggravation of defending a lawsuit, even if the Act is ultimately found to bar a judgment. At its worst, the Act may actually guide a plaintiff on how to draft technically adequate causes of action, thus allowing the case to survive possible legitimate challenges early in an action and embroiling volunteers in expensive and protracted litigation."[51]

State Laws Limiting Liability

"In addition to the Volunteer Protection Act, most states have some sort of provision that purports to limit the liability of directors on nonprofits. However, these statutes again generally do as much harm as they do good, by:

1) giving the charity a feeling of immunity when none is likely to exist, and
2) providing a roadmap to anyone suing as to what they need to allege.

"These statutes do not prevent the lawsuit from being filed, even if the directors are ultimately found to be protected by the statute. Since much of the cost of the suit is in the defense, there is often a large fee due to the attorney, even if you win. And, of course, there is no guarantee of winning.

"Let's look, for example, at the Florida law[52] to see how this works. The statute starts out by saying:

"(1) An officer or director of a nonprofit organization recognized under §501(c)(3) or §501(c)(4) or §501(c)(6) of the Internal Revenue Code of 1986, as amended, or of an agricultural or a horticultural organization recognized under §501(c)(5) of the Internal Revenue Code of 1986, as amended, is not personally liable for monetary damages...

Note: the insertion of 'monetary' would imply that there may be nonmonetary damages for which the director could be held liable.

"to any person for any statement, vote, decision, or failure to take an action, regarding organizational management or policy by an officer or director....

"If I were suing, one of the first things I would allege is that the matter decided by the officer or director that caused the damage had nothing to do with 'organizational management or policy,' whatever that is.

unless. . .

51. Chapter 33, "Volunteer Protection Act of 1997—An Imperfect Solution," *Nonprofit Governance and Management*, American Bar Association, 2002, for a more detailed explanation of this law.
52. See Florida Statutes Section 617.0834.

"Oh, yes. The 'unless.' This means that there is more below that I can allege on behalf of my client.

(a) The officer or director breached or failed to perform his duties as an officer or director; and

(b) The officer's or director's breach of, or failure to perform, his duties constitutes:

1. A violation of the criminal law, unless the officer or director had reasonable cause to believe his conduct was lawful or had no reasonable cause to believe his conduct was unlawful. A judgment or other final adjudication against an officer or director in any criminal proceeding for violation of the criminal law estops that officer or director from contesting the fact that his breach, or failure to perform, constitutes a violation of the criminal law, but does not estop the officer or director from establishing that he had reasonable cause to believe that his conduct was lawful or had no reasonable cause to believe that his conduct was unlawful;

"Well, let me see. My client is alleging sexual harassment, including unwanted touching. That would be a battery under criminal law, and those directors that allowed it—maybe they were aiding and abetting?

2. A transaction from which the officer or director derived an improper personal benefit, either directly or indirectly; or...

"What is an "improper" personal benefit? Is this opposed to a 'proper' personal benefit?

3. Recklessness or an act or omission which was committed in bad faith or with malicious purpose or in a manner exhibiting wanton and willful disregard of human rights, safety, or property.

"This is the provision you can drive a Mack truck through. As long as I plead recklessness, or bad faith, or malicious purpose (which of course they had, if they were so callous as to allow my client to be injured), or willful disregard for the safety and welfare of my client, I can always stay in court. You will not be likely to get out with a demurrer or even a motion for summary judgment.

"The point of this is to illustrate that, as I stated before, none of these statutes that limit liability prohibit lawsuits (which means that you still have to pay for a defense, even if you end up winning), areas where lawsuits are likely to happen are often excluded, and the law may simply provide a blueprint for anyone wanting to sue. Therefore, both indemnification provisions and a Directors and Officers Liability Insurance Policy (again, that covers the areas of likely suit) would be wise for a corporation to have."

Indemnification

"Okay, well that brings up the next item. Bill did point to the provision in our by-laws that says that the corporation will indemnify the officers and directors. I think that means that if we get sued, the corporation will defend us, rather than having to rely on insurance."

"Sam, how much money is in Save the Chipmunk's general fund right now that you could use for this purpose without affecting your programs?"

"When you put it that way, not much."

"Generally, indemnification statutes contain both mandatory and permissive indemnification provisions. Although the mandatory provisions are effective even if there is no language allowing indemnification in the bylaws, the permissive provisions are generally only effective if the board approves them. By providing for it in the bylaws ahead of time (i.e., providing for indemnification to the fullest extent permitted by law), you are making sure that the board does not vote against you when you need the indemnification.

"But indemnification is only as good as the organization. If the organization has no assets, then its promise to indemnify you is worthless. Further, sometimes there has to be an affirmative finding that you are entitled to the indemnification, and this finding must be made by a majority of disinterested directors. If a majority of the directors are being sued, then obtaining approval of a majority of disinterested directors becomes impossible. Further, plaintiffs may plead facts that, if true, would prohibit the corporation from indemnifying the director, and state statutes may require the director to successfully defend against the action before reimbursement is mandated, or even permissible.

"Incidentally, most of the lawsuits against directors involve employment issues (wrongful firing, discrimination, sexual harassment, etc.), so you should make sure that any D&O insurance policy covers these matters."

Employees and Volunteers

"Funny you should mention that. We recently had to let our secretary go. She was continually late, dressed totally inappropriately, chewed gum while she was talking on the phone, and was rude to one of our donors. We replaced her with someone who has actually been getting to work early, is nicely dressed, presents herself well, and really has seemed to be interested in the purposes of the organization. Yesterday we received a letter from an attorney for the secretary we let go, alleging wrongful termination and age discrimination. It is true that the first person was much older than the one we hired, but really we did not discriminate on the basis of age. Now what do we do?"

"Did you give her warnings before you fired her?"

"Well, every time she came in late, I confronted her and told her she needed to be on time. Once, when she was dressed as though she was going to the beach, I sent her home to change. But it was really her being rude to our donors that put it over the top. When this happened, I fired her the same day."

"Were any of your warnings in writing?"

"She had not been around long enough to have a formal review, so no."

"Was anyone else present when you provided the verbal warnings?"

"Generally I did it in my office, so I guess the answer is no."

"Sam, I am going to refer you to a labor lawyer who specializes in this type of law to defend you. The good news is that your state is an 'at will' state—you can hire and fire anyone for any reason at any time. But you need to understand that, since none of your warnings were in writing, if you are basing your decision on those various factors you mention, it will be your word against hers. Even with the donor—did you hear her being rude?"

"No, the donor told me. He was really upset with how he had been treated."

"So even in that instance, it is the donor's word against hers. She could claim that he misinterpreted her, or that she had not done it—that the donor just did not like her. The bottom line of all of this is, document, document, document."

How Should You Treat Your Employees?

The area in which directors and officers of nonprofits are most likely to be sued is the area of employment law—such matters as wrongful termination, sexual harassment, and discrimination. Many times those operating the nonprofit have thought that they were simply doing an individual a favor by paying him or her for odd jobs, only to find out that the courts were willing to grant the individual employee status and award him or her benefits far in excess of what the nonprofit anticipated.

A nonprofit is not exempt from most laws concerning employees. For example, the organization must withhold income taxes and Social Security taxes from the salaries, and pay the withheld amounts, along with the employer's contribution, to the state and federal government on a regular basis; it must comply with posting requirements; it must pay minimum wage to its employees; it must provide a safe working environment; and, depending upon the number of employees, it may be required to provide certain benefits such as maternity leave and family leave to its employees. An analysis (in fact, even a summary) of what these laws are and how they apply to a particular organization is beyond our purpose; any nonprofit that hires employees should take whatever steps are necessary to learn what these laws are and how to comply with them. Although there may be some differences from for-profit entities (especially with religious organizations), all employers must treat their employees in the manner the law requires.[53]

Having said this, there are some problems that are more likely to occur with nonprofit organizations. For example, one common problem is nonprofits that treat their employees as "one of the family." This may result in forgetting to do regular reviews of the employees (should be done at least annually). Or if reviews are done, the record is stated in a positive manner, rather than reflecting the areas that need change. The result is that when the person is finally fired, there is no supporting written documentation to back up the claims of the employer that the employee was consistently late to work, did not perform the work properly, and did not follow through on the areas that needed improvement. In employment law, perhaps

---

53   There are both federal and state employment laws about which the nonprofit will want to be informed. It is important to know what your state laws provide, as these are often stricter than the federal requirements, and can result in significant liability to the employer if violated.

more than any other area, as Sam is now finding out, it is important to remember that *if it isn't in writing, it doesn't exist* (or at least it will be difficult to prove).

Another problem that is perhaps unique to nonprofits is that they may expect the employee to "buy into" the core values of the organization. This can result in more involvement in the life of the employee than may be legally permissible. Generally, the organization has no control over the activities in which the employee can engage outside of work hours unless those activities directly affect the organization itself.[54]

Sexual Harassment Policy

"You mentioned sexual harassment. Do we legally need a sexual harassment policy? I know that the business I work for has one, but it doesn't really seem that important when we only have a few employees."

"Sam, the proper question is not, 'Do we legally need such a policy,' but, 'If I do not have such a policy, does this increase my risk of being sued, or of losing such a suit if and when it is brought?' The answer to the second question, even if you only have five employees, is YES!!!! The whole purpose of your organization having such a policy is to reduce your chance of being sued, and to give you some sort of defense if you are sued. In fact, even if you had no employees, it would be appropriate to have a sexual harassment policy because:

1. some of your volunteers could be regarded as employees; and
2. even if they are truly volunteers, they still might bring sexual harassment claims against the organization.

"The policy should apply to your employees, to your volunteers, and perhaps even to your constituents (there have been some cases where schools have been sued because of sexual harassment between students!)."

Employees v. Independent Contractors

"So, because of the potential problems with employees, Bill suggested that we might just want to treat everyone as independent contractors. Would that help?"

"No, Sam. That will probably get you into even more hot water. Someone must truly be an independent contractor in order to be classified as such. For example, an independent contractor is normally able to control how, where, and when they perform services for you, with you only being concerned about the end result. If you control the individual, including when, where, and how they do their job, that person is going to look like an employee. If they look like an employee, then you need to treat them as an employee."

Whenever a nonprofit organization is audited, the IRS will review the issue of misclassification of employees. The United States General Accounting Office estimates that the government loses billions of dollars annually as a result of the

---

54. Churches are a possible exception to this statement; they may require all of their employees to adhere to their doctrines. See Chapter 38, page 549, "Basic Corporate and Tax Aspects of Religious Corporations," *Nonprofit Governance and Management*, American Bar Association (2002).

misclassification of employees as independent contractors.[55] The IRS finds exempt organizations to contribute more than their fair share to this loss.

If your exempt organization has individuals being paid as independent contractors, you should look carefully at this area and determine if, following the common law guidelines, the individuals truly qualify as independent contractors. If an individual is not clearly an independent contractor, the organization can expect to be challenged in this area.

The place to start in an analysis of whether or not an individual should be treated as an employee would be with the common law employee test adopted by the Treasury Department:

> "Generally the relationship of employer and employee exists when the person for whom services are performed has the right to control and direct the individual who performs the services, not only as to the result to be accomplished by the work but also as to the details and means by which that result is accomplished. That is, an employee is subject to the will and control of the employer not only as to what shall be done but how it shall be done. In this connection, it is not necessary that the employer actually direct or control the manner in which the services are performed; it is sufficient if he has the right to do so. The right to discharge is also an important factor indicating that the person possessing that right is an employer. Other factors characteristic of an employer, but not necessarily present in every case, are the furnishing of tools and the furnishing of a place to work to the individual who performs the services. In general, if an individual is subject to the control or direction of another merely as to the result to be accomplished by the work and not as to the means and methods for accomplishing the result, he is not an employee."[56]

In doubtful cases, the determination will be made upon an examination of the particular facts of each case.

> "Facts that provide evidence of the degree of control and independence fall into three categories: behavioral control, financial control, and the type of relationship of the parties."[57]

Behavioral control includes:

1. Instructions such as:
   - When and where to do the work.
   - What tools or equipment to use.

---

55. Testimony of the United States General Accounting Office before the Subcommittee on Oversight, Committee on Ways and Means, reflects estimated losses in 1984 of $1.6 billion, in 1987 of $2.3 billion, and in 1992 of $3.3 billion. See GAO-T-GGD-196-130, page 5.

56. Treas. Reg. § 31.3401(c)1(b).

57. IRS Publication 15-A (Employer's Supplemental Tax Guide).

- What workers to hire or to assist with the work (the independent contractor can hire and supervise its own employees, but should not be supervised by, or supervise, the principal's employees).
- Where to purchase supplies and services.
- What work must be performed by a specified individual (employees generally are required to perform the services directly; independent contractors may often delegate).
- What order or sequence to follow.

The more that instructions are provided, the more the individual looks like an employee rather than an independent contractor.

2. Training. Generally, an organization trains its employees, whereas independent contractors bring the necessary skills with them, with no need of additional training.

Financial control includes:

1. The extent to which the worker has unreimbursed business expenses. An employee is normally reimbursed, while an independent contractor normally assumes the burden of his or her expenses.
2. The extent of the worker's investment.
3. The extent to which the worker makes services available to others, including whether they advertise, maintain a visible business location, and are available to work. Independent contractors generally are available to perform services for more than one entity.
4. How the business pays the worker. Although not always, an employee is generally guaranteed a regular wage amount for an hourly, weekly, or other period of time, whereas an independent contractor is often paid a flat fee for the job.
5. The extent to which the worker can realize a profit or loss. An independent contractor can make a profit or loss.

Facts that show the parties type of relationship include:

1. Written contracts that describe the relationship the parties intended to create.
2. Whether or not the business provides the worker with employee-type benefits, such as insurance, a pension plan, vacation pay, or sick pay.
3. The permanency of the relationship. The employer and employees have a continuing relationship, whereas an independent contractor works on a specified project or projects and then moves on.
4. The extent to which services performed by the worker are a key aspect of the regular business of the company. Employees' services generally are integrated into the organization's operations, e.g., their services are essential to bringing the employer's products or services to the marketplace. (This has become a major issue in some cases.)

Based on these factors, there are several practical items that the organization should have to support the position that someone is an independent contractor rather than an employee:

1. A written contract that reflects some if not all of the factors listed above and defines a specific project rather than an ongoing relationship.
2. A copy of the contractor's business license.
3. Bills sent to the organization on the contractor's letterhead rather than time cards.
4. The contractor having his or her own insurance.
5. A copy of advertising of the contractor offering his or her services to the general public (this could include the contractor's resume or curriculum vitae).
6. A copy of the contractor's business card.
7. A list of references of other businesses for which the contractor performs services.
8. In addition, the organization should deal with these individuals through the regular contract and procurement process, rather than through the personnel department.

Note that it is also important for the worker to have been consistently treated as an independent contractor, for the organization to treat others in a similar position in the same manner, for the organization to file all required federal tax forms (including Forms 1099), and for the organization to have a reasonable basis for treating the worker as an independent contractor.

What is the practical difference between treating someone as an employee rather than as an independent contractor?

1. Employees are required to report their annual compensation directly on Form 1040, and are generally reimbursed for expenses. They can claim unreimbursed business expenses on Schedule A only if they itemize deductions, and then only to the extent that such itemized expenses exceed 2% of adjusted gross income and are limited to claiming only 80% of business meals and entertainment expenses. Self-employed persons, on the other hand, report compensation and business expenses on Schedule C. Business expenses are deductible whether or not the individual itemizes deductions, and are not subject to the 2% floor, although they are also limited on the percentage of business meals that can be deducted.
2. Adjusted gross income tends to be higher if an individual reports as an employee, since unreimbursed business expenses are deductions from adjusted gross income. Self-employed persons deduct all business expenses in computing adjusted gross income. This adjusted gross income figure is important because the percentage limitations on charitable contributions and medical expense deductions are tied to adjusted gross income.
3. The forms used are different. Individuals should receive a Form W-2 each year if they are employees, and a Form 1099-MISC if they are self-employed.
4. Retirement benefits offered by some nonprofits may only be available to employees.
5. Disability pay exclusion is available only to those having "employee" status.
6. Once an "employee" status is adopted by issuance of a W-2 Form, it cannot be reversed in the eyes of the I.R.S.

"So I think you are telling me that a secretary will never be an independent contractor."

"Well, secretarial services may be performed by an independent contractor (for example, you might hire someone to send out a mailing to all your donors). But the secretary who comes in each day to answer your phone, open your mail, and type your letters is extremely unlikely to be anything but an employee."[58]

Can an Employee Volunteer Services to the Nonprofit?

"We have another issue as well. As I mentioned with our new secretary, she is very interested in what we are doing, and she has volunteered to donate back a certain portion of her time. So when she works 40 hours, we will pay her for 35. That isn't a problem, is it?"

"Oh, Sam. This is potentially even more of a problem than the independent contractor issue. Part of the problem is documenting that she is doing this voluntarily, and not because you asked her to. If she decides later that she was not treated correctly, she might bring an action for back wages. And if this results in her getting less than minimum wage, you may well find both the state and federal departments of labor getting involved."

This issue is found regularly with nonprofit organizations—where the employee may be either asked to volunteer his or her services, or where the employee may, at his or her own request, work additional hours at no charge.

All employees are either exempt or nonexempt with regard to overtime benefits, based upon the Federal Fair Labor Standards Act.

Nonexempt employees include all employees who are paid on an hourly basis and who are entitled to "overtime" benefits.

Exempt employees include certain officers, directors, managers, supervisors, professional and administrative personnel who are paid on a salary basis but who are not entitled to "overtime" benefits.

If the employee is an exempt employee, his or her job description can include duties that may require more than 40 hours per week of service. However, if the employee can perform the assigned duties in less than 40 hours per week, the employee cannot be penalized for working less than 40 hours, but must be paid his or her full salary.

If the employee is nonexempt, he or she must be paid for ALL work performed. Even if the nonexempt employee is normally paid a salary, if the employee works more than 40 hours, the employee must receive additional compensation for the overtime work. An organization CANNOT require a nonexempt employee to perform "volunteer" work for which the employee is not paid.

When any nonexempt employee, such as the secretary asks to be allowed to perform volunteer services, the organization needs to make sure that the employee is not somehow being pressured into performing these services. In addition, it would be wise to require that any volunteer services be outside of the normal course and

---

58. Recent IRS CPE addressing employer classification and withholding issues can be found at http://www.irs.gov/pub/irs—1tege/eotopicd03.pdf.

scope of employment (i.e., as the employee is a secretary, perhaps she could volunteer in a different capacity, such as leading nature walks)."

What Is the Difference Between a Volunteer and an Employee?

This also brings up the question of what, exactly, the difference is between a volunteer and an employee. Many nonprofits rely, in large part, on volunteers to staff their operations. Without volunteers, a substantial number of these nonprofits would be unable to perform at their current level of service. As a result, the use of volunteers has continued to be important to the charitable organization.

Essentially, a volunteer is someone who is entitled to no compensation and receives no compensation from an organization, is not reliant on the organization for sustenance,[59] and performs services out of the individual's own free will and not out of compulsion.

If compensation of any sort is received, then the individual is likely to be treated as an employee, subject to minimum wage and hour laws, and other requirements that attach to being an employee—including a requirement that the individual be covered by workers compensation. Along with this would be a requirement that the benefits received be treated as taxable income to the employee.

And if the organization is relying on the volunteer exception from unrelated business income tax, this exception disappears, which may result in taxable income to the organization.

Compensation does not have to be in the form of monetary remuneration.

A significant case in this area is the *Tony and Susan Alamo Foundation*[60] case, decided by the United States Supreme Court in 1985. The U.S. Secretary of Labor sued a nonprofit organization for violating the minimum wage, overtime, and recordkeeping provisions of the Fair Labor Standards Act (FLSA).

Benefits (food, clothing, shelter, and other benefits) were provided to the workers. This, along with the commercial nature of the work, appears to be crucial to the court's decision.[61] The receipt of benefits removed the workers from the status of volunteers, payment of benefits put the operations in line with the purposes of the FLSA, and the commercial activities removed the activities from the category of religious activities that might otherwise have constitutional protection.

The court did not prohibit volunteers with regard to religious activities:

> "It is clear, on the one hand, that an individual such as a prosperous lawyer ringing the bell for the Salvation Army on the street at Christmas time for a few hours is not an 'employee,' but a volunteer donating his time to the advancement of a worthy cause.... Yet it is equally clear that there comes

---

59. See, e.g., *Tony and Susan Alamo Foundation v. Secretary of Labor*, (1985) 471 U.S. 290.

60. *Id.*

61. The work being done by the purported volunteers in this case included working at service stations, retail clothing and grocery outlets, hog farms, roofing and electrical construction companies, a recordkeeping company, a motel, and companies engaged in the production and distribution of candy. at 292.

a time when secular endeavor must be recognized as such, and passes over the line separating it from the sacred functions of religious worship."[62]

However, the individuals in Alamo were working on a regular long-term basis *to survive*, rather than just volunteering a small part of their time. And the fact that the work was done for a commercial purpose is a continuing point emphasized by the court. In other words, if one engages in a commercial activity, then one will be subject to the same standards as anyone else. This last point is especially important today with the continuing complaints by businesses that nonprofit corporations are competing unfairly with them. The same drive to increase the scope of the unrelated business income tax is likely to demand that all other standards to which they are subject be imposed upon competing nonprofit organizations as well.

State law often also supports this position. In fact, state law may impose even stricter requirements than Federal law.

There are two reasons given for minimum labor standards: 1) to protect employees, and 2) to protect other employers that comply. Even if the employee consents to working for less than minimum wage, the state will *not permit* it. Calling an individual a volunteer will not change the requirement to pay an employee the minimum wage for *all* hours worked.

On the other hand, some individuals who are receiving compensation may still not be considered employees, because they are beneficiaries of the rehabilitation services being offered by the nonprofit organization. Under this argument, the person is admitted to the rehabilitation program for treatment. Any work therapy was performed to assist him in his rehabilitation, rather than to pay for his room, board, and clothing. But this only works if there is a structured program in place, and this is unlikely to be applied to individual cases where an individual is hired as an act of charity.

What Should You Know about the Use of Volunteers?

There are several areas of risk with the use of volunteers. The first is the risk to the organization itself from volunteer activities. If the volunteer is found to be performing services on behalf of the organization (especially if done at the direction of the organization), the organization may be liable for any resulting harm. There are several things that the organization should do to limit its liability:

1. Obtain insurance to cover the activities of the organization and its volunteers.
2. Proper screening of the individual (especially if the volunteer is to work with children). This can include making sure the individual is properly licensed and insured for the work performed.
3. A volunteer program, which identifies how an individual becomes a volunteer and outlines the specific areas in which volunteers are used. This will reduce claims that an individual was acting as a volunteer for your organization when the organization had no knowledge of his or her activities. In addition,

---

62. *Id.* at 399.

each volunteer should agree, in writing, that he or she will abide by all of the policies of the nonprofit.

4. Sufficient supervision for volunteer activities. This may include training, where necessary, and discipline or removal of the volunteer if any red flags are raised about the volunteer's performance. Be aware that the same liability for actions of employees may attach to actions of volunteers (e.g., sexual harassment).

Another area of risk is the risk to the volunteer. Your volunteers may find themselves at the center of a lawsuit when they thought they were doing good works. This often includes volunteers who are serving as directors and officers. Clearly, the organization should provide insurance protection and possible indemnification (see discussion, above).

There is another potentially significant issue that comes up if the volunteer is not an employee. If the individual is an employee, anything the employee creates as part of his or her employment belongs to the employer. However, if the individual is a volunteer, then what the volunteer creates belongs to the volunteer, unless the person has first signed a "work made for hire" agreement. This agreement should be obtained before the item is created. This applies anytime something creative is developed, such as a logo, photograph, web site design, document, or other "creative" work.

"That means we have a problem."

"What would that be, Sam?"

"Well, we had a volunteer design our logo. Does that mean that the logo does not belong to us?"

"You may have an implied right to use it, but you should see if the volunteer is willing to sign a document after the fact to clarify your rights. Although it is too late to get a work made for hire agreement, you may be able to obtain an assignment of copyright rights. This gives you most of the rights you would have under a work made for hire agreement, although there are certain residual rights that cannot be assigned."

"Okay, I will do that."

PART III

End of Life Planning for Exempt Organizations

After many years of hard work, at their last meeting the directors of Save the Chipmunks decided that it was time to call it quits. The chipmunk population in many states had expanded to the point that no one today would consider chipmunks to be endangered. Further, it was becoming harder and harder to obtain contributions. Even those individuals who had been among the largest givers over the years were turning their attention to other projects. And Sam, after many years at the helm, decided last year to retire. The remaining directors asked their consultant, Chip Finder, to explore the options of what to do with the nonprofit and to report back to them at their next meeting. Chip has asked Alvin for advice. What should Alvin tell him?

Options

When the members or directors of an exempt organization determine that it is no longer in their best interests to continue to operate as they have, there are several options open to them. If they want to continue in some fashion, it might be appropriate to expand the purposes—for example, Save the Chipmunks might be expanded to a larger purpose, such as, "Save the Rodents," or to something similar, such as, "Save the Lemmings." It might also be possible to reduce the size of the operations to fit with the current level of funding.

In most situations, however, when the directors decide that the corporation can no longer function in its current status, they do not want to resurrect it in a different form; they would prefer to be done with it. The options include merger with another exempt entity, dissolution and distribution of assets to one or more exempt entities, or transfer of control. Merger and dissolution involve many of the same steps, although dissolution is the most extreme change.

Both merger and dissolution of a corporation are accomplished pursuant to the state statute under which the corporation was incorporated. Dissolution in most states is relatively straightforward, although some states have made the process increasingly difficult. The following is a generalized discussion; it should be noted that there may be additional requirements in some states that are not set forth below. It should also be noted that there may be some differences, based on the type of exempt organization (for example, mutual benefit corporations are generally not subject to the review of the Attorney General unless they hold assets in charitable trust).

If a merger is possible, the corporate purpose may be able to be continued, albeit in a modified form. Some of the existing members (or directors) may wish to serve in the surviving corporation, thus continuing their oversight over the assets. This may be desirable, especially if a stronger capital base is needed.

Another option would be to keep the organization separate, but to have another group take over the control by being elected to a majority of the board positions or a majority of the membership. Alternatively, the assets might be distributed to another entity, keeping the current entity shell alive for use at a later date.

One item to note: If a corporation merges with another entity, under most corporate laws, the surviving entity will normally be the recipient of any bequests to the merged entity. There is no similar provision for a corporation that receives the assets of a dissolving corporation. Therefore, if the disappearing corporation has done a good job of convincing people to include it as a beneficiary under their wills or trusts, merger should be strongly considered. On the other hand, in a merger, the acquiring entity receives all of the assets *and liabilities* of the merging corporation. Therefore, if the liabilities (including contingent liabilities) exceed the assets without some other corresponding benefit, dissolution and distribution of any remaining assets, after payment of creditors, might be preferable.

Sale of Assets

If the corporation sells all or substantially all of its assets, it must first get approval from the directors, members (if any), and other persons specified in the organization's Articles. In addition, approval may need to be obtained from the government entity responsible for oversight of charitable organizations. For example, in California, charitable organizations must provide written notice to the Attorney General.

Conversions

A corporation may convert into any other type of corporation by amending its articles. In some states, entities, including corporations, limited liability companies and partnerships, may also be able to convert into another type of entity. The corporation's board, its members, if any, and any other person whose approval is required by the articles must approve the change. If the organization has assets, the government entity responsible for charitable oversight must approve any change of a charitable entity into a business entity form.

Having said all of that, it must be emphasized that assets subject to a charitable trust must continue to be used for the purpose for which they were given. Therefore, if the purpose of the organization changes significantly, steps must be taken to assure this use. For example, at the time of the conversion, if a charity converts into a business entity, there must be a transfer to a similar nonprofit exempt organization of assets equal to the value of the organization.

Transfer of Control

Sometimes those involved with the organization determine that they are no longer able to operate the organization effectively; however, there may be others who would be willing to take control of the organization and continue its operations. For example, Joe's Home for Delinquent Boys might be willing to take over the control the operation of a home for girls when the individuals operating that home are no longer willing or able to continue. However, because the home for girls may have a somewhat different purpose, rather than merging the two organizations, the board of the home for girls might resign after having elected the directors of Joe's Home for Delinquent Boys as their replacements. The directors could then determine the best structure for the two corporations. For example, they might rewrite the bylaws so that the directors of Joe's Home for Delinquent Boys serve as the members and choose the directors of the home for girls.

Steps for Voluntary Dissolutions

There are several steps that may need to be taken in order to dissolve a nonprofit corporation, including:

1. The directors of the organization should vote to wind up and dissolve, and adopt a plan of distribution (e.g., who gets the assets). If the organization is a charity, this will normally be another charitable entity with similar purposes. If the organization is a mutual benefit organization, such as a social club or a condominium homeowners association, the assets may go to the members. One should review the articles to determine if there is a dissolution provision that states what happens to the assets upon dissolution.

2. The members of the organization, if any, and any other persons specified in the Articles, should vote to wind up and dissolve.

3. An initial notice of election to dissolve may need to be signed by the president and secretary and filed with the Secretary of State's office. This step is not required of most states.

4. Preapproval from the IRS might be required before making fundamental changes. This is especially important if the organization is a private foundation.

5. Let your creditors know what you are doing, and either pay them off or have the organization taking over your assets assume the liabilities. If there are any contingent liabilities, notice of the dissolution should be given to each possible creditor and perhaps published in a newspaper of general circulation. This notice may require a claim to be filed within the requisite time period. If no claim is filed, depending upon the state law, the claim may be barred. If the state law does not provide for a method to limit con-

tingent liabilities, or if the creditor was not correctly notified, the creditor may be able to file a claim against the recipient of the assets, up to the amount of assets received.

6. If the corporation is a charitable entity, approval for the transfer of these assets may have to be obtained from the government entity regulating charitable assets.

7. A filing may also have to be made with the state taxing authority.

8. All assets of a charitable entity that remain after payment of liabilities must be distributed to another exempt organization. The organization(s) to receive the assets should be similar to the organization being dissolved, and may be specifically designated in the Articles.

9. When the assets are distributed, a Certificate of Dissolution, which must be signed by the directors of the organization, will then filed with the Secretary of State's office. In many states, this is the only filing required.

   One should note that in many states, the law currently applicable to nonprofit organizations may not be the law that was effective at the time the organization was formed. This may lead to confusion, both on the part of the applicant and of the state examiner, as to the exact requirements for dissolution.

10. Some states also require that there be a notice of dissolution published in a local newspaper of general circulation to complete the dissolution process.

11. If the organization is required to file informational returns with the IRS, it must file a final informational return and include a copy of the Certificate of Dissolution and any other information required by the IRS. Final state informational returns may also be necessary.

Steps for Mergers

The steps to merge two nonprofit corporations are very similar:

1. The terms of a merger agreement must be negotiated. It is important that the purpose of each organization be similar enough that the assets of the disappearing organization will continue to be used for a similar purpose. Items that might be included in a merger agreement include whether or not members of the disappearing organization become members of the surviving organization; whether or not any of the directors or officers of the disappearing organization become directors or officers of the surviving corporation; changes to the articles or bylaws; and possible restrictions on the use of assets.

2. The directors of each organization should vote to merge and approve the merger agreement. This should be done in accordance with the terms of their respective bylaws.

3. The members, if any, of each organization should vote to merge and approve the merger agreement. Again, this should be done in accordance with the terms of their respective bylaws and the laws of the state of organization. Sometimes the members of the merging corporation may become members of the surviving corporation; any such provision should be contained in the merger agreement.

4. The merger agreement should then be signed by the president and secretary of each corporation and filed with the Secretary of State's office.

5. Preapproval from the IRS might be required before making fundamental changes. This is especially important if the organization is a private foundation.

6. Approval for the merger may need to be obtained from the government entity regulating charitable entities, and possibly from the state taxing authority.

7. Once the requisite approvals are obtained, the merger agreement will be filed with the Secretary of State, and the merger will be completed.

Note: No notice to creditors is required in a merger. This is because any liabilities of the disappearing corporation are assumed by the surviving corporation as part of the merger.

There may also be other filings that should be made. For example, the surviving organization might want to file to protect the use of any names that had been used by the disappearing organization. If the disappearing corporation was incorporated or qualified to do business in states other than the surviving organization, the surviving organization may want to refile in those states. Finally, some licenses do not automatically transfer from the disappearing organization to the surviving organization. It is good practice to check with any state regulatory authorities through which the disappearing organization is licensed BEFORE the merger, to see if any filings are necessary to transfer such licenses.

If the merger is between corporations in two different states, care should be taken in drafting the merger agreement to make sure it complies with the requirements of each state law. The merger agreement will then be filed with the Secretary of State or equivalent entity in both states. As the merger agreement will indicate which is the surviving corporation, after the agreement is filed in each state, the state in which the surviving corporation is located will have complete authority over the merged entity.

Practical Questions to Ask

After listening to Alvin's recitation of this information, Chip Finder has realized that, to advise the board of Save the Chipmunks of the best solution, he needs to find out what exactly the board wants and what the current status of the corporation is. For example:

1. Do any of the members/directors wish to continue to operate a similar nonprofit corporation? If yes, the choices should include options for continued involvement, such as expanding the purpose, or merging with a nonprofit that would agree to this involvement (such as by adding one or more directors to their board, etc.).
2. Are there other nonprofits in existence with similar purposes that would be interested in merging, or with which Save the Chipmunks would want to merge?
3. Does the corporation have significant bequests? If yes, strongly consider merger over dissolution.
4. Does the corporation have significant liabilities, possibly in excess of assets (including contingent liabilities)? If so, dissolution might be the best option, with notice given to all creditors and potential creditors.
5. Is there an organization that would like to acquire the assets, perhaps by purchasing the same? This would be helpful if the liabilities are significant.
6. Are there specific 501(c)(3) organizations that the members or directors would like to see benefited upon the dissolution of Save the Chipmunks? Note: The Attorney General will be concerned if significant assets will go to an organization with purposes unlike those of Save the Chipmunks. Further, this option may be limited if the Articles list the distributees.
7. Are there any gifts with reverter clauses?
8. Is there a time frame by which the board would like to see this accomplished? Are there ongoing expenses that need to be eliminated?
9. Is a health facility involved? If so, the government is likely to take a much more active role in reviewing and approving any transfer of assets.
10. Is anyone going to object to the disappearance of Save the Chipmunks?
11. Is there an organization or other individuals that would like to take over the operation of Save the Chipmunks?
12. Is there dissension about this matter that might require the involvement of the court?

Once the board has thought through where they are now and where they really want to end up, then they will be able to make a decision of how to get there.

Special Considerations of Membership Organizations

"This must be my month for dissolutions," Alvin commented to Sam Goodman, who had come in to have his estate plan reviewed.

"Interesting you would say that. My church is now trying to decide what steps it should take. I don't know if you remember, but the Oak Street Church is in an urban area, and most of the people who have been longstanding members have moved out of the area with their families. Those of us who are left have had to take up special offerings just to keep the roof from falling in."

"So are you thinking of dissolving?"

"We aren't sure what to do, but we know we need to do something."

"You know, of course, that the assets must be used to advance the purposes for which the church was formed. Therefore, the overriding question is whether the church, as it is currently situated, can effectively continue to carry out its purpose. If it cannot, then a decision must be made that will allow the assets to be used in a way that does advance this purpose."

"You have hit the nail on the head. It seems clear that the church is not effectively ministering to the remaining members, much less new individuals, since our numbers keep diminishing. Even Ruth, one of our oldest board members, does not really want to continue to attend. And the chance of attracting a significant number of new members to a dying church located in a depressed area (especially members with money) appears to be small. If we cannot attract enough members to support the facility, our only hope would be to borrow the money needed to keep the facility in good repair. I have told them that they are only postponing the inevitable, in a way that will result in a reduction of the assets that the church has."

"Quite right, Sam. Maybe you could suggest they consider one of the following solutions:

1. Sell the current facility, and lease or purchase a smaller facility in the neighborhood that the current members can afford. In fact, you might find another church that would be willing to buy the property and lease part of it back to the church. This will immediately reduce the overhead, and will also make funds available to actually expand the ministry, or to support another ministry in a more viable area. However, there is no assurance that the current members will remain, especially if some already want to leave. The same problems now being faced might be faced again in a few years. However, if a number of the members are elderly and unable to drive to a new location, keeping a church presence in the area may be found to be essential to the well being of the remaining members.

2. Merge the church with another church in the area, selling one of the facilities and keeping the one most suitable. This would increase membership of the remaining church and decrease the expenses of keeping two churches open. Again, with this choice, the money received from the sale can either be used to continue the ministry of the surviving church, or could be contributed to assist another church in an area where the former members are now living and attending church. The downside of this choice is that mergers result in two pastors with competing objectives (e.g., keeping their jobs). Also, sometimes with this type of merger, the congregation of the church facility that is kept feels that the church continues to belong to them, and that the new members are intruders who must conform to their practices. If this attitude is taken, it will only succeed in driving the members of the merged church away and will not result in any long-term benefits.

3. Find an additional nonprofit or two that might want to lease a portion of the facility from you. Of course, if you do this, you will continue to be responsible for the facility and its upkeep, and you may still not get enough money to pay for the repairs needed.

4. Dissolve the church, and let the members attend other, more thriving churches. If this is done, the assets, upon payment of the debts of the church, must be distributed to another nonprofit organization with the same or similar purposes (e.g., another similar church, preferably one nearby). Sometimes the articles or bylaws specify the organization(s) to receive the assets upon dissolution.

"Two other questions, however, must be asked before the decision is made:

1. What do the members want? Generally, the members of a church congregation have input in the decision, and they should be consulted before the final decision is made. Clearly they have an interest that must be taken into account before a decision is made.

2. If the church is a part of a denomination, what does the overseeing church entity want to see done? Often, with denominational churches, the local church cannot make the decision alone. Before the directors make a final decision, either or both of these groups should be consulted."

"Alvin, I have another question: I am concerned that the members and directors may all resign before this is completed. What will happen then?"

"Depending upon state law, the last director may not be able to resign unless someone else is found to take over the responsibility. Someone will have to remain in charge."

"So if I don't want to be the one turning out the lights, I better not be the last one to resign."

"Right again, Sam."

Appendix A

SAVE THE CHIPMUNKS
CONFLICTS OF INTEREST POLICY[1]

Article I

Purpose

The purpose of this conflicts of interest policy is to protect the interest of SAVE THE CHIPMUNKS (the "Organization") when it is contemplating entering into a transaction or arrangement that might benefit the private interest of an officer or director of the Organization or might result in a possible excess benefit transaction. This policy is intended to supplement but not replace any applicable state and federal laws governing conflicts of interest applicable to nonprofit and charitable organizations.

Article II

Definitions

1. Interested Person
    Any director, principal officer, or member of a committee with board-delegated powers, who has a direct or indirect Interest, as defined below, is an Interested Person.
2. Interest
    A person has an Interest if the person, directly or indirectly, through business, investment, or family:
    a.   has an ownership or investment interest in any entity with which the Organization has a transaction or arrangement;
    b. has a compensation arrangement with the Organization or with any entity or individual with which the Organization has a transaction or arrangement;

---

[1]. This policy is drafted for directors and officers. The organization may wish to consider adopting a similar policy for employees and/or volunteers.

c. has a potential ownership or investment interest in, or compensation arrangement with, any entity or individual with which the Organization is negotiating a transaction or arrangement;

d. is a member, director or officer of an organization with which the Organization has entered into or is contemplating entering into a transaction or arrangement;

e. [other situation where a conflict of interest may arise with the organization].

Compensation includes direct and indirect remuneration as well as significant gifts, favors, or contributions.

An Interest is not necessarily a conflict of interest. Under Article III, Section 2, a person who has an Interest may have a conflict of interest only if the appropriate board or committee decides that a conflict of interest exists. A transaction is not prohibited simply because a conflict of interest exists.

Article III

Procedures

1. Duty to Disclose

    In connection with any actual or possible conflicts of interest, an Interested Person must disclose the existence of his or her Interest and must be given the opportunity to disclose all material facts to the directors [or members of committees with governing board delegated powers] considering the proposed transaction or arrangement.

2. Determining Whether a Conflict of Interest Exists

    After disclosure of the Interest and all material facts, and after any discussion with the Interested Person, the Interested Person will leave the meeting while the determination of a conflict of interest is discussed and voted upon. The remaining directors [or committee members] will decide if a conflict of interest exists.

3. Procedures for Addressing the Conflict of Interest

    a. An Interested Person may make a presentation at the board or committee meeting, but after such presentation, he or she will leave the meeting during the discussion of, and the vote on, the transaction or arrangement involving the possible conflict of interest.

    b. The chair of the board or committee will, if appropriate, appoint a disinterested person or committee to investigate alternatives to the proposed transaction or arrangement.

    c. After exercising due diligence, the board or committee will determine whether the Organization can obtain, with reasonable efforts, a more advantageous transaction or arrangement from a person or entity that would not give rise to a conflict of interest.

    d. If a more advantageous transaction or arrangement is not reasonably possible under circumstances not producing a conflict of interest, the board or committee will determine by a majority vote of the disinterested directors whether the transaction or arrangement is in the Organization's best interest, for its own benefit, and fair and reasonable to the Organization. It will make its decision as to whether to enter into the transaction or arrangement in conformity with such determination.

OTHER PROVISIONS SPECIFIC TO THE ENTITY—the following is an example:
If the Interest involves a loan to an organization and
(i) an Officer or Director is a member, director, or officer of the organization, the loan must be approved by either the Board Loan Committee or the full Board of Directors in full compliance with this Policy.
(ii) a Director is a member, director, or officer of the organization and is a member of the Board Loan Committee, the loan must be approved by the full Board of Directors in compliance with this Policy.

4. Violations of the Conflicts of Interest Policy
   a. If the board or committee has reasonable cause to believe that a person has failed to disclose an actual or possible conflict of interest, it will inform the person of the basis for such belief and afford the person an opportunity to explain the alleged failure to disclose.
   b. If, after hearing the response of the person and making such further investigation as may be warranted in the circumstances, the board or committee determines that the person has in fact failed to disclose an actual or possible conflict of interest, it will take appropriate disciplinary and corrective action.

Article IV

Records of Proceedings

The minutes of the board and all committees with board-delegated powers will contain:

1. the names of the persons who disclosed or otherwise were found to have an Interest in connection with an actual or possible conflict of interest, the nature of the Interest, any action taken to determine whether a conflict of interest was present, and the board's or committee's decision as to whether a conflict of interest in fact existed;
2. the names of the persons who were present for discussions and votes relating to the transaction or arrangement, the content of the discussion, including any alternatives to the proposed transaction or arrangement, and a record of any votes taken in connection with the proceedings.

Article V

Compensation

1. A voting member of the board of directors who receives compensation, directly or indirectly, from the Organization for services is precluded from voting on matters pertaining to that member's compensation.
2. A voting member of any committee whose jurisdiction includes compensation matters and who receives compensation, directly or indirectly, from the

Organization for services is precluded from voting on matters pertaining to that member's compensation.

3. Individuals who receive compensation directly from the Organization, whether as employees or independent contractors, are precluded from membership on any committee whose jurisdiction includes compensation matters.

4. Procedure for Establishing Compensation of Interested Persons

   a. An Interested Person may provide information to the board or committee, but after any such presentation, he or she will leave the meeting during the discussion of and the vote on compensation.

   b. Compensation will be approved by the board or a committee of the board that is composed entirely of individuals unrelated to and not subject to the control of the Interested Person whose compensation is being determined.

   c. The board or committee will obtain and rely upon appropriate data as to comparability of compensation, including but not limited to such things as:

      (i) compensation levels paid by similarly situated organizations, both taxable and tax-exempt, for functionally comparable positions;

      (ii) the location of the organization, including the availability of similar specialties in the geographic area;

      (iii) independent compensation surveys by nationally recognized independent firms; and

      (iv) actual written offers from similar institutions competing for the services of the Interested Person.

   d. The board or committee will document the basis for its determination, which documentation will be made a part of the permanent minutes and records of the board or committee.

Article VI

Annual Statements

Each director, principal officer, and member of a committee with governing board-delegated powers will annually sign a statement that affirms that such person:

a. has received a copy of this conflicts of interest policy,

b. has read and understands the policy,

c. has agreed to comply with the policy,

d. has disclosed all known actual and possible conflicts of interest involving such person and his or her family members, and

e. understands that the Organization is charitable and that in order to maintain its federal tax exemption it must engage primarily in activities that accomplish one or more of its tax-exempt purposes.

Article VII

Periodic Reviews

To ensure that the Organization operates in a manner consistent with its charitable purposes and does not engage in activities that could jeopardize its tax-exempt status, periodic reviews will be conducted. The periodic reviews will, at a minimum, include the following subjects:

a. whether compensation arrangements and benefits are reasonable, based on competent survey information, and are the result of arm's length bargaining;
b. whether acquisitions of services result in inurement or impermissible private benefit;
c. whether partnerships, joint ventures, and arrangements with management organizations conform to the Organization's written policies, are properly recorded, reflect reasonable investments or payments for goods and services, further the Organization's charitable purposes and do not result in inurement, impermissible private benefit, or an excess benefit transaction;
d. whether agreements for services and agreements with Organizations, employees, and third party payers further the Organization's charitable purposes and do not result in inurement, impermissible private benefit, or an excess benefit transaction.

Article VIII

Use of Outside Experts

When conducting the periodic reviews provided for in Article VII, the Organization may, but need not, use outside advisors. If outside experts are used, their use will not relieve the board of its responsibility for ensuring that periodic reviews are conducted.

SAVE THE CHIPMUNKS (the "Organization") CONFLICTS OF INTEREST STATEMENT

In order to assure that the highest standards of ethical and fiduciary standards are maintained by SAVE THE CHIPMUNKS, I, _____ (print full name), a board member and/or officer (circle one or both) of the Organization, affirm that:

a. I received a copy of the Organization's Conflicts of Interest Policy.
b. I read and understand the Policy.
c. I agree to comply with the Policy.
e. I understand that SAVE THE CHIPMUNKS is a charitable organization and that in order to maintain its federal tax exemption, it must engage primarily in activities that accomplish one or more of its tax-exempt purposes.

My Residence/Contact Information is as follows:

Name: _____

Address: _____

City/State/Zip: _____

Telephone: _____

Fax: _____

Email:

My Employer is:

Employer Name
(if self-employed/
retired, so state):
Address: _____

City/State/Zip: _____

Telephone: _____

Fax: _____

Email:

   I am/was a leadership person, board member, committee member, member or employee of the following additional organizations similar to or affiliated with SAVE THE CHIPMUNKS:

Org Name/Position: _____

Org Name/Position: _____

Org Name/Position: _____

Org Name/Position:

   Please continue with additional positions on separate paper if necessary.
   Finally, I affirm that, except as described herein, to the best of my knowledge, neither I nor any of my family members* are now or have been at any time during the past year:

1. a participant, directly or indirectly, in any arrangement, agreement, investment, or other activity with any vendor, supplier, or other party doing business with the Organization which has resulted or could result in personal benefit to me/him/her;
2. a recipient, directly or indirectly, of any salary payments, loans, significant gifts, free services or discounts, or other fees from or on behalf of any person or organization engaged in any transactions with the Organization.

Exceptions: _____

_____

_____

_____

_____

*Family members include: spouse, parents, siblings, children, step-relations, and in-laws.

In the interest of full and complete disclosure, list anything that might possibly be a concern of which the SAVE THE CHIPMUNKS board should be aware:

Item #1: _____

Item #2: _____

Item #3: _____

Item #4:

Please continue with additional items on a separate paper, if necessary

I declare under the penalty of perjury under the laws of the State of California that the foregoing is true and correct and that this declaration was executed on _____(date) at _____ ___ (location).

_____
(Signature)

Appendix B

ADDITIONAL RESOURCES

General

Guidebook for Directors of Nonprofit Corporations, 2nd Edition, ABA, Section of Business Law, published 2002.

Nonprofit Governance and Management, ABA, Section of Business Law, published 2002.

Materials resulting from a joint effort with the ABA's Tax Section, Business Law Section's Nonprofit Committee and Commission on Racial and Ethnic Diversity within the Profession—The Tax Exempt Toolkit—can be found on the ABA Tax Section's home page at http://www.abanet.org/tax/. Click on Tax Tips 4 U, then scroll down to the Tax Exempt Toolkit.

Other helpful articles may be found at http://www.runquist.com/articles.htm.

Numerous listservs, archived comments, and other materials can be accessed through http://CharityChannel.com/.

See the Council on Foundations, http://www.cof.org for articles targeted at private and community foundations.

National Center on Philanthropy and the Law at NYU, http://www.law.nyu.edu/ncpl/libframe.html.

See also Don Kramer's Nonprofit Issues, http://www.nonprofitissues.com.

The IRS website contains a number of useful articles concerning exempt organizations. See http://www.irs.ustreas.gov/charities/index.html.

Board Governance

Help 4 NonProfits & Tribes, http://www.Help4NonProfits.com.

For additional tools, help-sheets, and articles aimed at boards, see Nathan Garber & Associates, http://garberconsulting.com.

For Canadian associations, see http://www.axi.ca/services/resources.htm.

Employment

Recent IRS CPE addressing employer classification and withholding issues can be found at http://www.irs.gov/pub/irs-tege/eotopicd03.pdf.

Intermediate Sanctions

Bruce Hopkins, The Law of Intermediate Sanctions, 2003, John Wiley & Sons, Inc.
Recent IRS CPE on Intermediate Sanctions, http://www.irs.gov/pub/irs-tege/eotopice03.pdf.

Insurance

See Nonprofit Risk Management Center, http://nonprofitrisk.org, *and* http://www.insurance-fornonprofits.org.

Joint Ventures

Joint Ventures Involving Tax-Exempt Organizations, 2nd Edition, 2000 by Michael I. Sanders, John Wiley & Sons, Inc.

Planned Giving

Planned Giving Resources, http://www.pgresources.com/regs.html.
The Complete Guide to Planned Giving, by Debra Ashton, http://www.debraashton.com.
Gift and Estate Resources for Professionals, http://www.gift-estate.com.
Planned Giving Design Center, http://www.pgdc.com/usa/
National Committee on Planned Giving, http://www.ncpg.org.

Lobbying and Political Activities

Recent IRS Published Guidance on Political Activities: http://www.irs.gov/pub/irs-drop/rr-04-6.pdf.
Recent IRS CPE on Political Activities of 501(c)(4)s, (5)s and (6)s, http://www.irs.gov/pub/irs-tege/eotopicl03.pdf.
The IRS's Comprehensive CPE on Political Activities, in Q&A format: http://www.irs.gov/pub/irs-tege/topici02.pdf. *The Federal Election Commission (note especially the campaign guides, and links to laws):* www.fec.gov.
The Alliance for Justice http://www.allianceforjustice.org/nonprofit *contains resources concerning nonprofit advocacy activities.*

About the Author

Lisa A. Runquist is a partner in the law firm of Runquist & Zybach LLP, with offices in California and Washington. She has over 25 years of experience representing nonprofit organizations and is the first winner of the Outstanding Lawyer Award, a Nonprofit Lawyers Award presented by ABA Business Law Section. She has authored numerous publications on nonprofit and religious organizations and has been active in nonprofit and exempt organization committees of both the American Bar Association and the State Bar of California.